SPICY TASTY
VEGAN CUISINE
"EAT YOUR WAY TO A HEALTHY LIFE"

ALL RECIPES ARE VEGAN, GLUTEN-FREE & NON-SOY!

MAMA NAASIRA AGEELA & DR. GREGORY JOE BLEDSOE

SPICY TASTY VEGAN CUISINE

"EAT AND HEAL AT THE SAME TIME"

Mama Naasira Ageela &
Dr. Gregory Joe Bledsoe, J.D.

Copyright 2015 by Naasira Ageela and Gregory Joe Bledsoe
Source Of Light Publishing
P.O. Box 27504 • Oakland, CA 94602
www.spicytastyvegan.com
spicytastyvegan@gmail.com
Phone: 510-473-6579

ISBN #978-1515305293

All rights reserved. No part of this book may be reproduced, stored in retrieval system, scanned, or transmitted in any form or by any means – electronic, mechanical, recording, photocopying, or otherwise – without permission of the authors.

Book Design by black ink + paper
Photography by Jamil Wallace & Naasira Ageela
Edited by Mary Anne McNease
Editor Assistants: Mardeen Cassell, Drexel Lyles, Linda Odumade
Subtitle Quote from Thelma Carrington

Book Layout ©2015 black ink + paper

Notice: The information contained in this book is for educational purposes only; it should not be used for diagnosis or to guide treatment without the opinion of a health professional. Any reader who is concerned about his/her health should contact their Health Care Practitioner.

Ordering Information: Quantity sales. Special discounts are available on quantity purchases by corporations, associations, and others. For details, contact the "Special Sales Department" at the address above.

Special thanks to the Most High (our Ancestors, Mother/Father God, Divine Spirit) and all the others who, without their love, inspiration, information and guidance this book would not be. Below are listed some of the individuals and businesses we would like to recognize for their support. This list is far from complete.

Ruthie Mae Fletcher (Mom)
Mary Anne McNease
Chamaine Woffard
Caroline & Richard Cannon
Rev. Diana McDaniels
David de la Vega
Kimone Gooden
Olric Carter
Howard & Claudette Morrison
Josefa Perez
Rainbow Grocery – San Francisco
William Taylor, Esq.
Dr. Delbert Blair
Dr. Veronica Hunnicut
Rev. Eloise Oliver
Dr. Christopher Kox
Harold Manley
Barbara & Truman Hildreth
Jamil Wallace
Atiba Wallace
Dulani Wallace
Thelma Carrington
Henry Crater
Marilynne Davis
Alton Byrd
Michele McKenzie

JacQueene Hedquist
Brotha Ra
Diana Lynch
Nubia Sutton
Leonard Franklin
Barbara Bridgewater
Pio Winston
Bonnie Strong
Kristin Graetz
Carol Jean Jones
Fevn Cintron
Far–I Shields
Elaine Shelly
Veronica Butler
Anna Marie Coleman
Dr. Gail Meyers
Ms. Tessie Bledsoe
Virna Tarvarez
Roselind Hildreth
Areca Smit
James Sandoval
Rebecca Clemons
Rose Joyner
Herma Jean Gardere
Monique Levi
Debra Jones-Davis
Miliani Wallace
Gracie Taylor

Contents

Naasira Ageela's Introduction 5
Transitioning to Healthy Foods 7
Testimonials 9
Storage Containers 25
Basic Kitchen Safety Tips 31
Naasira's Approach 35
Recipes 45
Spicy African Stew 46
Almond Arugula Pesto 51
Almond Coconut Date Rolls 52
Almond Banana Smoothie 53
Almond Milk 54
Baked Butternut Squash 55
Baked French Fries 56
Banana Fruit Cookies 57
Banana Fruit Loaf 59
Blueberry Almond Butter Smoothie 61
Wild Rice 62
Citrus Drink 63
Cocoa Mousse 64
Collard Green Wraps 65
Wrap Sauce: 67
Vegan Real Cornbread 68
Daikon Kale Stir-Fry 69
Earthy Root Detox Tea 70
Egg Substitute 70
Fruit Grain Cereal 71

Simple African Fufu	72
Shallot Popcorn	73
Tasty Guacamole	74
Natural Hair Conditioner	75
Hemp/Basil Dressing	76
Hemp Milk	77
Kale Chips	78
Simple Kale Stir-Fry	79
Lasagna with Basil Cashew Cheese	80
Tasty Millet	84
NaaCereal	85
Quinoa, Black and Red Rice Mix	87
Real Banana Pancakes	89
Pineapple Rind Drink	91
Pizza	92
Plant Protein Filling	94
Spicy Vegan Plantain	96
Tasty Polenta	97
Portobello Mushrooms	98
Tasty Potato Salad	99
Pulp Burger/Juice	101
Raw Ice Cream	102
Raw Salad	103
Vegan Real Waffles	104
Roasted Eggplant Vegetable Casserole	106
Salad Dressing	108
Steel Cut Oats	109
Baked Sweet Potatoes/Yams	110
Quinoa Tabouli	111
Mixed Spiced Tossed Salad	112
Variety Fruit Salad	113

PART 1

CHAPTER 1

Naasira Ageela's Introduction

IT IS AMAZING WHEN you can live long enough to learn there are many realities to life. I am happy today to have learned there is a more natural and sustainable diet to nurture the body. I learned to care for my health by getting sick and then reading and asking questions to help myself get better. If you know and believe natural remedies will help you feel better, instinctually you will explore other options.

If I had not contracted Hepatitis B from sticking myself with a needle, while working as a phlebotomist at the UCSF Medical Center at the tender age of nineteen, I would not be living the healthy, vibrant, invigorating, creative life I enjoy today. That needle stick turned out to be a divine blessing.

When I became ill, I had no idea that the food we ate was supposed to nourish our bodies.

My doctor warned me that if I wanted to live, I would have to change my diet. The candy and fast food had to go. I began researching healthy foods and so embarked on my journey from illness to wellness. I discovered the healing properties of fruits and vegetables, grains, herbs and spices. Where I lived was brimming with restaurants, health food stores and fruit stands, and I learned new and different ways to make healthy meals without meat.

What started out as a misfortune, became my great fortune. I have been blessed in many ways by the benefits of eating a healthy diet and have become part of a wonderful community along the way. Twelve years ago, I became a vegan and was honored to share my vegan cooking experience with Gregory Joe Bledsoe and others through our cooking classes.

What we endeavor to do in this book is share our knowledge and passion for life, learning and abundant health. It's not just knowing enough to get by, not just making do, not settling for less, but expanding, growing, sharing, supporting each other and re-creating our community. I accepted my calling to prepare spicy, tasty food to remain healthy and to support the folks who are interested in being healthy as well.

We have learned over a period of sixty years that the words we use are powerful. It is so important to watch what we say. Words can enslave, words can empower and everything in between. Think of your words as electromagnetic boomerangs that you throw and that come right back to you. Another way of putting it is – put good stuff in, get good stuff out. Like cooking, like life. I know I am so thankful for the many gifts I have been blessed with and grateful to be able to share with others who are open to receive them. Hopefully, the ideas and information in this book will help you in your journey, wherever it takes you. Be healthy, be well, my friends!

CHAPTER 2
Transitioning to Healthy Foods

ONCE YOU DECIDE TO make a transition to healthy foods, the first thing to do is to list all of the foods and drinks you are currently consuming that are unhealthy for you. Then, next to each unhealthy food or drink, write in the name of a healthy alternative. At your own pace, substitute out the unhealthy foods and drinks by replacing them with more healthy alternatives.

An example would be to "substitute out" drinking cow's milk by replacing it with almond or hemp milk. The almond and hemp milk is certainly healthier for most. You can also make the hemp and almond milk yourself. Another example would be to replace vegetable oils with extra virgin olive oil or raw coconut oil (especially for high heat cooking). Continue to "substitute out" until your list of unhealthy foods has been completely replaced with healthy alternatives.

Remember, it took a lifetime for you to get where you are today. But the time it will take for you to transition to optimum health can be relatively short. Your motivation will be the way you look and feel. As you eat better, you think and can do better. Just as one must take a step to begin a mile journey, you can begin your journey to eating healthy foods by switching, one at a time, unhealthy choices for healthy ones.

Also, it is important to keep in mind that as you change your diet and lifestyle your body will begin to detoxify. This means, your body will start to eliminate toxins. Generally, this is done through your bowels cleaning out and becoming more regular.

CHAPTER 3
Testimonials

When you eat something Naasira and Gregory Joe have made, you can actually taste their spirit. They are akin to modern day explorers on a treasure hunt for optimal health and wellness.

–Areca Smit, Oakland, CA

It is with great pleasure that I applaud Gregory and Naasira on the exceptional work they have done in showing Americans how to prepare and enjoy vegan cuisine. Their food is healthy and delicious! What a blessing this couple is to all of us!

–Dr. Veronica Hunnicutt, San Francisco, CA

For meat eaters, they will not be dissatisfied. The seasonings are wonderful. I have experiences with many vegetarian restaurants and much vegetarian cuisine and I can say without a doubt that Greg and Naasira's recipes are wonderful.

–Mali Vincent Williams, Oakland, CA

If you thought meat WAS good, try this alternative. You will be hooked for life.

–Hajjah Roslyn Abdullah, Oakland,CA

A culinary magician, Naasira's cooking is simply magical. As a born soul food meat eater I appreciate texture, seasoning, variety and ultimately a filling meal. I have found all of the above in Naasira's vegan dishes. Among the many dishes she creates, her stews, salads and cornbread stand out as the best dishes I have ever eaten. They burst with flavor engulfing all of the senses in a melody of Caribbean, African, Asian, and Eastern taste, all carefully balanced by deliciousness.

Her dishes are hearty and they have the power to lure, cure and win over even the most skeptical eaters. Eating her dishes made me realize that even I could become a vegan and eat fulfilling foods that are both satisfying and healthy. One taste is all it takes to realize a glimpse of heaven is attainable by tasting Naasira's dishes.

–Dr. Shaute Tosten, Temecula, CA

Every time I taste or experience Naasira's food I get an electric charge going through my body. I have never tasted food that lifts my vibration that high. I would recommend this book to anyone and everyone who is sick and tired of being sick and tired.

–Nubia I, Oakland, CA

Delicious! The food is a life changing experience. It's new and fresh. It is the total opposite of a hard brick in the stomach feeling after eating a double cheeseburger that is hard to digest.

–Ms. Tessie Bledsoe, Las Vegas, N.V.

A new definition of what eating is ... a combination of herbs and spices on veggies that speak a new language of pure goodness to your inner being. This is vegan fuel that lights you up like an old fashioned pinball machine. It is a twist and shout of flavor to a vegan vegetarian cuisine. The taste is truly a hallelujah moment.

–Dr. A.B.Bruce, D.C., Stockton, CA

Sistah Naasira and Brotha Greg's food is very nutritious, delicious and satisfying. It's prepared in a clean environment with love, wisdom, and "overstanding". On the benefits of their foods: It cleans the colon. Thus, helping to prevent colon cancer. The food has the natural vitamins the body needs to maintain good health and longevity. Try it. You will love it. It's good for you and refreshing too.

–Raslam Atiba, Oakland, CA

Naasira's food is nourishment for the soul. More than just a meal, it satisfies desires you didn't even know you had! Every time I eat her food it realigns my body, mind and spirit in new ways and I gain energy and reach new levels of clarity. To call her a chef is an understatement. She is a healer using food as medicinal alchemy. She truly embodies the spirit of how to eat to live.

–Zakiya Harris, Visionary, Catalyst, Cultivator, Oakland, CA

This is good and nutritious food without the salt, sugar and grease. When you finish eating you feel like you've been nourished. This book is back to the essentials of healthy eating. This is medicinal food with love.

–Leon Williams, Berkeley, CA

I really enjoyed the African Stew dish. It has a variety of vegetables and spices. This particular dish has given me more energy to help deal with my asthma. Thank you and congratulations on this book.

–Shelby Hammonds, Daly City, CA

When she put the plate in front of me I said "What a plate." It was tasty. She used a lot of herbs and spices. It was healing. It was a meal where you just wanted to savor the flavor.

After eating I felt the food healing me or giving a positive healing effect. I did not feel bloated or stuffed. I felt great. I also really enjoyed the collard green wraps.

–Khatia Washington, Columbia, MD

My girlfriend and I have known Greg and Naasira as a couple for ten years. Years ago, we started stir-frying our vegetables the way Greg and Naasira showed the two of us. We have become healthier (I have lost twenty pounds and still, to this date, continue to lose weight). As the result of the more healthy way of cooking and eating a vegetable-based diet, our lives have certainly been enriched.

The two of us are grateful for Greg and Naasira, vegans, and advocates for a vegetable based diet. Their passion for a healthier way of living has touched the lives of so many people. May they continue to be blessed as they continue to be a blessing to so many people through their healthy cooking.

–Stephen Nunley and Katrytae McCraw, Fremont, CA

My testimony is on the pulp sandwich: Now some people would think, how in the world could a sandwich made of pulp be inviting? Let the truth be told, this sandwich was outstanding!

It is very flavorful and filling (I got full, and I can eat!). This sandwich contains the pulp of all the healthy foods like carrots, celery, beets, pineapple, and so on. It was topped off with mustard, catsup and avocado.

It was also like bringing your health and five senses back to life while eating. You could enjoy this sandwich and get a raw detox at the same time. This was a seriously healthy MAN'S sandwich.

Bro. Karl Grant, El Sobrante, CA

Naasira and Greg are on a mission to improve the health of their community one meal at a time. These recipes are not only good for you, they're also good to you.

–Michele, CA

Naasira and Gregory's delectable creations have nourished and comforted me for years. They consistently remind me of the importance of taking the time to prepare wholesome, tasty meals. It is such a gift that they are sharing their recipes, which I feel are relatively easy to prepare and offer healthy and hearty vegan options. Naasira and Gregory also have an immense understanding of the many facets that contribute to good health. I consider them to be wonderful resources and examples of healthy living in general.

–Jamillah Sabry, Oakland, CA

Delicious, wholesome, and absolutely filling epitomizes this vegan cuisine. The soups and stews delight your palate with a rich and robust mixture of spices, topped off with a homemade spread on pita bread creates a dish fit for a king, queen, or family. Contrary to your mother's twist on it, their homemade pizza is amazing and a must for gatherings both, small or large. Trust me, your guests will thank you for it!

My favorite, however, is the fruitbread. With four different flours and every fruit you can imagine, you won't be able to take a bite without devouring a wealth of fruit.

Although sweet, this organic desert is going to be one of the best vegan goodies you'll ever have! All the recipes within this cookbook are life giving, healing, and have assisted me on my journey of healthy eating and living. So begin yours today!

–Vanessa Dilworth, Oakland, CA

The Vegan Love Doctors Naasira and Gregory Joe are the ones I refer to when my body is in need of some medicinal cleansing and healing with food. One of my favorites is their pulp sandwich and beet juice. I believe that we must have a relationship with the food we choose to put in our bodies. Their food makes this relationship a loving, spiritual and healthy connection. Vegan love forever.

–Margo Harper, San Pablo, CA

The food that Naasira has cooked for me is super fantastic. It's the type of food that gives one a long life expectancy. I call it my healing food and the way that it is prepared is simply amazing. You have every root and herb and vegetable known to man and the way it's prepared and the mixture of it is outstanding. I call Naasira my vegan queen. It's amazing how she knows how to prepare the right types of food for any type of ailment that one may be experiencing in their bodies.

Once you have a mindset to eat properly and eat what God has put on this earth for us to digest and to eliminate in the proper way, we find ourselves having more energy and your thinking capacity is very clear. So, I must say you can't lose with the stuff my vegan queen does use.

–Deborah Benefield, Oakland, CA

Proper eating, Dr. Joe says, is one of the secrets of life. I agree and the vegan vegetarian cuisine is very good and truely "soul" food. The waffles were excellent! They were a lot better than mine. They are a part of a fabulous vegan cuisine by people who are very conscious about their diet. And thanks to Dr. Joe I am now getting back into the waffle game in a more healthy way.

–Leonard Franklin. Oakland, CA

One of my favorites is Naasira's Guacamole. It is "the bomb", "to die for". The vegan popcorn with garlic, cumin, and the many spices is wonderful. When I want to eat something sweet, this is the thing to eat. It is so much better for you. It keeps me from eating anything that is sweet that I should not eat and it is very delicious. This is cooking that will embrace you when you have the mind–set for living a healthy, longer and productive life. You will feel great too!

–Diana Lynch, Oakland, CA

I have dined on their delicious vegan meals and it has really made a believer out of me that vegetables and spices can be combined in such a way that it can tantalize your palate and make you want more and more. I have eaten pulp sandwiches that were just fabulous made from the remnants they utilize of what was not cooked up into their delectable dishes. They are also so delicious and delightful to the palate as well.

−Marilyn Richburg–Reynolds, Oakland, CA

I think it is a wonderful thing that we have decided that the way we used to eat is really not healthy and that we have people such as Naasira and Greg that take the expressed time not only to cook the right foods and be healthy, but to teach everyone else how to do it. I think that it's extremely important that we do this and they walk as superior examples that we are what we eat and we should eat well so we can look well.

−Rhonda Crane, Oakland, CA

I love the taste and the flavors. It is good and it makes you feel good. I wish I could eat like this all the time.

Teresa Daigle, San Pablo, CA

The fruitbread is delicious and amazing. I never expected vegan food to be so filling, satisfying and yummy.

−Stephanie DeVito, Oakland, CA

Because I was privileged to have access to Naasira's health sustaining foods, my vitality and overall sense of wellbeing has increased. The foods and recipes along with their good water and exercise have helped to stabilize my health.

−Harold Manley, Age 82, Claremont, CA

I had the awesome pleasure of not only dining on some of Gregory and Naasira's delectable cuisine, but watching them prepare it as well. It was total Love in action. Their food is thoroughly satisfying not only for the body, but the soul and mind as well. I know if we took all of Gregory and Naasira's healing advice and ate the way they suggest, the world would be in a much healthier place. I thank God for these two angels. Peace and Blessings.

−Rebecca Clemons, Oakland, CA

For a couple of years Naasira served up a variety of recipes, which she was developing and testing, to the delight of many who worked at the City College of San Francisco Libraries. I was the beneficiary of great and wonderful, natural whole foods, both raw and cooked, which surprised the palate by many subtle flavors from start to finish, and satisfied the body's needs no less than the soul. A meal from Naasira's cuisine was never short of color, texture, flavor, love and good will. I treasure the memory and crave the cooking.

−Dr.Christopher Kox Interim Dean, Library City College of San Francisco

I have had Naasira's vegan breakfast meals. They are nourishing, filling and delicious. Sometimes when you are trying to eat healthy some of the foods may not taste good. But this is not the case with Naasira's food. It is very tasty. I would eat a half bowl of the breakfast cereal and eat the other half the following day. Everything that should be in a good healthy breakfast meal was in it. There are raisins, fruits, oats, and vegetables. The fiber has helped improve my digestive system and the meals gave me more energy. After eating the breakfast, I would feel good all over. Naasira's breakfast food really put me on the road to healthy eating.

–Phyliss McFee, Oakland, CA

Naasira's food is a miracle. I once had a stomachache for about a week. I ate some of the vegetable stew, cornbread, salad and collard green wraps. Suddenly, my stomachache was gone. When I was sick with the flu I drank some of her citrus drink. It gave me energy and I felt so much better. I could drink it every day. Her smoothies are also amazing. Her food is natural, medicinal and tasty. I can feel the energy flowing through my body as I eat it.

–Marissa Tampoya, Oakland, CA

I love them. Their food is food of knowledge, learning, healing and love.

–Herma Jean Gardere, Richmond, CA

I used to work with Dr. Bledsoe at a junior high school in Oakland, California. I had the opportunity to inquire about why he had so much energy, was always so slim, very active and very alert all the time. He was one of the teachers that never got sick. If he took off it was because he was planning something else. But he was never sick, which raised my curiosity about his diet.

I had the pleasure of tasting the breakfast made of quinoa, different types of rice, vegetables and fruits with superfoods. I had never tasted it before. But it was delicious. I really enjoyed the breakfast. I felt a sense of wellbeing without being full. It was very tasty, especially for me, not being accustomed to quinoa.

I told my sister about it and she was so curious that she started to order the quinoa breakfast. She also had that sense of wellbeing and wanted to continue ordering that special recipe which was very tasty. I continued eating the breakfast and always felt so energized knowing I was eating clean organic food.

I highly recommend this new cookbook and any of the recipes. They are 100% organic and most of all are healthy and very good for you.

–Yolanda Carrillo, Daly City, CA

I have known Gregory for the past five years. And I have enjoyed his recipes and his advice in the field of healing. This has helped me physically to overcome illnesses. Gregory also strengthens my knowledge of self–healing through natural foods.

–Kareem Zuniga, born in Guatemala, Central America, currently residing in Oakland, CA

Naasira and Dr. Bledsoe may not fully realize how significantly they made a difference in my life. They helped me change the way I eat. It really does take a village! Thanks. –Greg McNamara, Placerville, CA

I want to express my appreciation for the wonderful things Naasira and Gregory have done and the beautiful menu they have created. I didn't know very much about vegan or vegetarian food. But thanks to them a whole new world has been opened. They have prepared meals showing how delicious this food could actually taste. The food is prepared in such a way that it is attractive, smells good, and it is good for you. That is a delightful combination. Thanks again for showing us a better way of eating. –Anna Coleman, Long Beach, CA

I first experienced Naasira's excellent food a year ago. Leftovers left too soon. When I found out they were coming back to the DMV. I had to set up a chance to allow good vegetarian friends to experience this wonderful banquet of love, taste and color. Every one at Eden Valley was overjoyed. We all ate ourselves blissful. I look forward for the ability to take Naasira's recipes and attempt to create a feast 1/3 as delicious as hers because I know 100% is impossible.

–Drexel Lyles, Washington, D.C.

I really appreciate the vegan food. The wholesomeness has helped heal me in my sicker days and helped give me vitality. I recommend all of these recipes to each and every one to help you become more whole and also have a tasty time doing it.

–Alton, CA

I am privileged to have met Naasira and Dr. Joe (Gregory Joe). I met Naasira while working at the Rosenberg Library at City College San Francisco. She introduced me to some of her smoothies and vegan food. The smoothies gave me such a boost of energy it was like I was running around cleaning up the building. The stress of my job seemed to go away. I had so much energy I started each day walking a mile around the college track. I no longer had the cravings to eat the chips and junk food that I had eaten before.

Being a carnivore, I had no idea food without meat could taste so good. I have eaten everything they have fixed for me. It is so hearty and filling. After eating it I feel like I am on cloud nine. I now make my own smoothies two to three times a week. It helps keep my energy up and tastes great too. My experience with Naasira and Dr. Joe's smoothies and food has changed my life for the better. I am no longer anemic nor a borderline diabetic.

–Doretha Evans, San Leandro, CA

With the help of Naasira's food I have changed my diet. By changing my diet to vegan I can truly admit that this is the best way to go. I feel great. I look great. This is the best I have felt in over 10 years. Change your diet and you will live a lot longer.

–Sharon Yasin, San Francisco, CA

As a friend and supporter I have gained from your superb efforts, knowledge and sacrifices in bringing forth your outstanding wisdom and life saving recipes. Your work has resulted in me improving my eating habits and becoming self-educated about what to eat and how to eat to live. My whole hearted thanks are due to the both of you who are truly One. Congratulations! Its time the world knows real truth and real Love.

–JacQueene Hedquist, Las Vegas, NV

The cornbread is excellent. My son loves it. He is always asking me when I am going to make more. I am so glad that Naasira and Greg are caring and sharing this wonderful way of eating. The food is good to you and better for you.

Thelma Carrington, Age 83, Okemah, OK

Naasira is very passionate about the vegan lifestyle and healthy eating. She is very knowledgeable about what ingredients are necessary for an authentic vegan dish. Furthermore, Naasira understands what foods are required for healing and nourishment for the body. I will definitely continue to use her recipes on my voyage to a healthy lifestyle.

–Lakysha Cummings, Oakland, CA

I can always speak about Sister Naasira's vegan cuisine with sheer delight because it is both delicious and life saving. One day Naasira entered the classroom with an aroma that had entered before her. The fresh healing smell let me know this was the way to go. It was appetizing, flavorful and magnificent to the body, mind and soul.

Under the presence of her food you quickly are made aware just from the smell alone it has healing qualities to both the spirit and the body. This makes her food nurturing love in action.

My favorite foods are her wonderful sandwiches. The pulp and humus sandwiches are simply amazing. And...Oh my God!, the stir-fry. It is a variety of spices combined with moist vegetables bursting with flavor. Each and every bite is an experience you will not forget.

Naasira's fine preparation of food has taught me that if I change the way I eat, I will change the way I heal.

–Linda D. Lovett, San Bernardino, CA

Dr. Bledsoe and his wife Naasira have provided incredible inspiration for my eating habits and me. When I first met Dr. B, at the middle school where I currently work, I was a full-blown meat-eating carnivore. I was sluggish and would routinely get tired and fatigued throughout the day, which is a huge problem when you work with teenagers. I would see how Dr. B was so energetic and enthusiastic throughout the day and decided to talk with him about how he maintains his high energy. He told *me about his vegan diet and healthy eating habits. He then began to bring me a smoothie every morning.*

Not only did I find myself feeling better and having more energy, but also they tasted delicious! After this experience I began to do some research into the factory farm system in this country. I read a book called Eating Animals by Jonathan Safran Foer and The Omnivore's Dilemma by Michael Pollan. Both of these books along with my conversations with Dr. B convinced me to change my eating habits and become a vegetarian.

This was the best decision of my life. It was over three years ago and I have not looked back. I've never felt better! I have energy throughout the day, I feel more clear-headed and my immune system has vastly improved. In fact, I cannot remember the last time I was sick and I am around "germ factories" all day! I am forever grateful to Dr. B and Naasira for providing a wonderful model of healthy living and showing me that a vegetarian/vegan diet can be not only very satisfying but extremely tasty as well.

–Nicholas Miller, Oakland, CA

I really love the salads Naasira makes. Eating her salads changed my way of eating. They are wonderful. I loved them so much I had to ask her to make me some every week. I never had any type of salads like those before. I love the colorful variety of vegetables. The salads are very natural with good nutrients you can feel going through your body. The fruitbread is the BOMB too. You cannot find food like this on the open market. I am waiting for Naasira and Dr. Joe to open a restaurant so I can daily eat her delicious healthy food.

–Lawrence Reese, San Francisco, CA

Naasira and Dr. Joe have recipes that support your immune system, which promotes a hearty healthy thyroid. This is one of the major concerns of many African American women. Armed with love, a cozy kitchen and a genuine traditional African concern for authentic foods, they are on a single mission to promote healthy eating lifestyles.

They teach cooking and eating the way we need to know. Both Naasira and Dr. Joe compliment each other in their joint effort to promote healthy eating. Naasira's gourmet style embraces Dr. Joe's support and inspiration.

They are true representatives in letting "food be their medicine, and their medicine be their food". They both illuminate great health. Whether raw or freshly cooked vegan dishes, they are both joined at the apron in demonstrating a healthy and better alternative to the way most of us have eaten. They are a sweet couple deserving a "Best Seller". Love, peace and blessings,

–Aminah Huang, Oakland, CA

Naasira's food is easy to eat. It is very tasty, nutritious, good for you and your digestive system. It is a great colon cleanser. I mean, it really helps to clean you out. I also enjoy her smoothies that seem to be made with love and magic.

–Donna White and Ferondus Ellis, Richmond and Emeryville, CA

2014 is the year of vegan cooking. This cookbook is a must to have because these recipes are extraordinary. I ate Naasira's food for seven days. My digestive system was much better. My bowel movements improved. My skin looked better and my eye stopped twitching. Eating Naasira's food was detoxing me as I dined on her delicious, nutritional cuisine.

–Rahima DuBose, Atlanta, GA

I was born and raised in San Francisco. Somehow, I ended up in Point Hope, Alaska. Like most, I eat some good food. But most of it is really not good for me at all. Not too long ago I came down from Alaska. My sister hooked me up with some of her mean, lean, vegan cuisine. In the short time I was there I could tell the difference. Her food really lifted me up. I could feel it go through my entire body. I could tell that this is the way I should be eating. My wife also likes the food. Naasira's cooking has inspired me to change my diet.

–Richard Cannon, Point Hope, AK

I came home real tired one day. I started eating some of Naasira's stew. I enjoyed the taste. It warmed my body and made me feel better. I do like the stew!

–Cynthia Taylor, Treasure Island, CA

Last year, I pulled a muscle in my stomach. The doctors didn't seem to know what was going on. But I did know that I was sick. I had been in the house for 17 days. I had lost 40 pounds. I could not eat, nor hold anything down. I was "toe up". Then my wife appeared like an angel with Naasira's food. It was one of the best stews I have ever eaten. It was prepared well. The salad was good and healthy. It was the only food I was able to keep down at the time. I ate it for 3–4 days.

After eating Naasira's food I felt so much better. I am now off the medication and a lot of unhealthy stuff. Whatever it is that she puts in her stews does the trick. I would recommend her recipes for anybody.

–Ken Taylor, Treasure Island, CA

I love Naasira's food. It doesn't just push you out and make you feel fat and all like that. I especially enjoyed the breakfast Gregory made. It was delicious.

–Ruthie May Fletcher, Age 85, Las Vegas, NV

Nutritional is a word that is used by many chefs and cooks all over the world. I believe most of them only speak about these values from the point of the foods they prepare.

But Naasira and Gregory's food hold the nutritional value and taste that allow our bodies to do all the talking.

I am a survivor of Type 2 Diabetes. I had struggled with many years of pains and inconsistency with my sugar levels. Let's put it this way, I love food! For years I would consume any dish that was put in front of me, even if it wasn't good for my body. I was raised on Naasira's food and because of this my body was never subjected to any major illnesses during my youth and adolescence.

As a young man from twenty to twenty eight years, my ignorance to the blissful consumption of the unnecessary would steer me to those burger and fries, "we all love so much". I felt prescribed medicine would have done more damage to me only because I was on the border of being a Type 1 Diabetic. I was afraid that if I took the medicine, I would have been much more careless about the foods I consumed and my illness would eventually accelerate.

Pain would strike constantly in my legs, feet, and joints. I would even have problems with my vision. Then I came home, I tasted Naasira and Gregory's food for the first time. I say it was my first time only because my eyes were finally opened and I could see clearly. The freshness of their organic salad's, soups, and smoothies give me all the nutritional value my body needed.

Thank you very much Naasira and Gregory for opening my eyes.

–Atiba Wallace, Anchorage, AK

Naasira and Dr. Joe make food for the Spirit. I have known them for going on two years and see them nearly every week at the farmer's market. I can attest to the fact that they are people who practice what they preach. That is, positivity, health, knowledge and love. Having tried a number of their always delicious and nutritious creations and knowing the love and care they put into all aspects of their lives, I have found myself highly anticipating the release of this book. It will be a welcomed and necessary addition to any kitchen.

–James Sandoval, Oakland, CA

I am truly a food connoisseur. I love to eat. I have eaten all kinds of food. I've eaten Indian, Greek, Italian, Japanese, Russian, Kosher and so many more. My favorite food is Naasira's for the following reasons. It is healthy and healing. It is filled with the best of herbs that Naasira has studied, thought about and figured out what they all are good for. In other words, which herbs were healing for the body, mind, and soul. I don't want you to take my word for it. Please, try it yourself.

My brother was in the hospital for over a month. I went to see him every day, two to three times. The only thing I could think of was getting him to eat Naasira's food when he got out of the hospital. Even if I would have to tie him up and put it down his throat, I was willing to do that. But as it turned out, he was willing to try it.

Thank God, within a week he was recovering well. I would say about 70% of the recovery was Naasira's food. The rest was lots of sleep and personal love and care from his daughter and me. So, I can say thank you Naasira and Greg for your support and always being there delivering the food and every delivery was different.

You will never find it being cooked the exact same way. It is always different and it gets better and better. It changes with the four seasons. I could go on and on (smile). But this is her book, not mine. I have been eating Naasira's food for about twenty-two years or more. It is the best thing that can happen to a human being. Thank you Naasira and Greg.

–Bonnie Strong, San Francisco, CA

My sister had recommended Naasira's cooking to me in an effort to get me healthier. I did not try her food until after my hospitalization. When in the hospital I ate food on the hospital menu, which included meat. After my hospital stay I discovered the benefits of Naasira's food with its many herbs and spices. Before eating Naasira's African stews and stir-fries, the medication I was taking seemed to drag me down. I seemed to have little or no energy. But Naasira's food made me feel better. I no longer had the desire to eat meat. I portion out the stew and eat it with my other food. It is a great pick-me-up. It has helped to boost my immune system and build up my body. I now feel so much better. In fact, I feel like a new person.

–Henry Crater, San Francisco, CA

I had cancer and was undergoing chemotherapy a few years ago. I did not go through what a lot of people went through. I mean, the throwing up. I did not go through any of that because of Naasira's food, citrus drink and tea. It kept my body cleansed. I had no poison backing up in my system.

The citrus drink is incredible! Whenever I would start to get a cold, congestion, or a sniffle I would drink it. The problem was gone. The cereal is good. The stew, with all those vegetables and spices is delicious. It includes turmeric, which is good for any inflammation in my body. My cancer in now gone and I appreciate Naasira for being there for me. –Maxine Dempsey, Oakland, CA

I would like to thank you and Joe for what you did to help my mother. I know what you did had an impact on my mother's recovery. I could feel the energy in the food and your citrus drink you gave her. When I saw my mother drinking the citrus drink, I had a cold and I wanted to give it a try. When I drank the citrus drink it heated my chest. Suddenly, everything came right out. The cold was gone. What you do is lovingly amazing.

–Bryant Dempsey, Stockton, CA

I'm no Foodee, but I thoroughly enjoyed the dish you guys prepared for me at lunchtime that day. You put it in a "to go" container allowing me to stay on schedule. That was love in true form. Thank you. Thank you very much. Your new creations with vegetables, oils, herbs and spices are so delicious, even sexy, that the taste stayed with me thoughout my day.

I know you two will continue this grand nutritional effort. We are what we eat and your creations will make us all better people. I miss our retirement planning sessions. You guys have arrived and are blessed. May God continue to bless you two.

–Tillman Pugh, MBA, CFP, Oakland, CA

After eating what Naasira and Gregory prepared I felt like Wow! Could this actually taste this good without meat? Keep in mind, I'm a true Inupiat, Eskimo from the Arctic of Alaska. In order to survive in this harsh environment we need protein (all our traditional food). But once I tasted the food I thought I could actually get use to this stuff and enjoy it at the same time, knowing all the nutritional benefits of the food. The salad was very delicious! When I see Naasira and Greg preparing the food I also see the energy and love that they put into it.

Had I not known them, with the energy they have, I honestly would have thought they were in their early forties. When actually, they are in their early sixties. That's living proof as to how healthy this food truly is. With that said, I highly recommend for everyone to check this food out.

–Caroline Cannon, Point Hope, Alaska

I had the opportunity of having Greg and Naasira visit me during the summer. They introduced me to their wonderful way of cooking. I watched both of them as they prepared their meals. I was fascinated as they took the time to intricately cut up each vegetable and herb.

I always tried to eat right. But watching them made me feel a little closer to healthy eating and living. I enjoyed the meals that included kale, greens, broccoli and cauliflower. Everything was fresh.

I also introduced this way of cooking to my grandchildren, ages 4 and 8. To my surprise they really enjoyed the vegetarian dishes. I now prepare vegan food most Sundays for them. At 63, I am very impressed with what I have learned from Greg and Naasira as I try this new way of eating. Thank you, Greg and Naasira.

–Kazzandra Greene, New York City

On the food preference continuum that extends from the carnivore on the right to vegan on the left, you two were always considered by me to be to the left of my fish and chicken diet. And, since getting joy out of eating is such a personal thing, I immediately felt a bit of trepidation upon receiving your invitation to sample your Food of Life. The trepidation came out of my respect for your culinary attainments and not wanting to make negative comments about your choice of foods.

[Background – I am not a gourmet. Therefore, whenever I dare to comment on some food I have been given, in all likelihood, I will be expressing to the inquisitor why my brain is processing – that my preferences in eating were either: not disturbed by this menu or that my preferences in eating were, in fact disturbed. The verbal expressions of those brain processes usually gets further reduced down to the words "I like it" or "I have problems with this." Rarely–to–never would I give any qualitative assessment of the food: I might get kicked out of the host's house]

So, when you gave me your Food of Life dishes, I felt a bit of trepidation. Very timidly, I opened the lids of your "to–go" containers, and immediately recognized the rice and the striking fresh salad. And surprise, surprise, once heated, the flavors of the main dish poured out and drove me to devour everything over the course of two days – except the avocado sandwich.

The salad was quite alive and included greens (as opposed to just lettuce), which greens proved to be a pleasant surprise. The dressing you provided was a revelation. The latent sweetness of the main dish (possibly from the tomatoes or their sauce) balanced the spicy rice quite nicely. The breakfast mix was used as ice cream scoop-sized balls along side my everyday breakfast fruit.

Thank you for opening my palate. Thank you for the deft touch of giving me "to–go" containers that allowed me to sneak a taste away from your public viewing. The superiority of the food gave me everything I would have had at a formal sit down dinner – except you watching me eat (again, the trepidation). Thanks again.

–William Taylor, Esq., Oakland, CA

I would like to sing my praises for the most delicious and remarkably nutritious fruitbread ever made. It is moist and sweet without the sugar or butter. This taste along with the nutritional qualities would never happen in regularly baked commercial goods. Vegan cooking and baking are pleasant surprises to the healthy side of culinary art. Thanks.

–Marguerite Versher, Oakland, CA

As a vegetarian for over 25 years and event planner for nearly 20 Collard Greens Cultural Festivals and Cook-Offs between California and Georgia, I believe I am well qualified to judge any collard green dish raw or cooked. The Collard Green Wrap – Um, Umm, Ummm. Absolutely delicious! It is a dish for any time of the day...breakfast, lunch, dinner or as a snack. Naasira and Greg are true food scientist. They know exactly what herbs and spices bring out the flavor of any vegetable. Eating their colorful and delicious meals prepares you for a healthy journey of peace, love and longevity.

"The Collard Green Queen"

–Dr. Mama Nobantu Ankoanda

The food was invigorating! The raw ingredients left me feeling energized and uplifted. It was like a pick-me-up food. The taste was delightfully wonderful, with a natural savory sweet taste. I felt the energy of the soul in the food. In all honestly, it was the best raw sandwich I have ever experienced.

I love you both. –Khadijah Grant, El Sobrante, CA

Naasira's Vegan dishes were always a hit when my student organization held events. The fresh salad and vegan pasta was delicious. I loved the sauce for the pasta, and so did everyone at the events. That is why it would be eaten very quickly. The food was truly appreciated by people of all cultures. It was a delight to serve food that not only satisfied your taste buds, but that was also good for those you are serving. After seeing how much people loved the vegan food from Naasira, I made sure to have some at every event.

–Jesse James, Sacramento, CA

I have known Naasira to be an excellent cook for all of the past forty years we have been friends. She always loved cooking, sharing her talents and family recipes, while taking excellent care of her children and overcoming personal health challenges. When she became a vegetarian and later a vegan, her passion increased and blossomed into an avenue for change in the community and the world, one person and one plate at a time. Her food is delicious, beautiful and healthy. What more can you ask food to be? Her partnership with Gregory has only added to her inventive spirit and her search for the truth. Their collaborative efforts are a gift to all who seek an enlightened awareness along with a healthy and happy tummy.

–Mardeen Cassell, Antioch, CA

I remember a time being very ill and Naasira's wonderful, wholesome food totally nourished me back to health very quickly. Naasira cooks soul food the way it should be. It is healthful as well as tasteful. I can only imagine how much healthier the black community and everyone else for that matter would be if they could cook food the way Naasira prepares it with her loving hands. The community would no longer battle health problems like obesity, high blood pressure, high cholesterol, etc. This is healing food and everyone would be blessed immensely to have the opportunity to taste Naasira's amazing cooking!

–Samantha Mathews, Istanbul, Turkey

No one else has done what MAMA Naasira and Dr. Joe have done to help improve my health. Since meeting them, I have had nothing but success with my health. I really appreciate the quality of their food. They used the highest quality ingredients of organic, unrefined unprocessed foods.

They uniquely prepare the food in a way that tastes like special gourmet meals, which is something not easy to do when preparing vegan food. When you eat their food you are eating close to the way God intended for us to eat. I feel they are closest to the creator in that sense.

I will continue to deal with them for my health. And I would also recommend to anybody and everybody that they should definitely buy their book and listen to what they have to say. It will make the quality of your life so much better.

–Anthony Edwards, San Leandro CA

One Friday afternoon I experienced a literal smorgasbord of vegetarian delight. It was delicious! I had a lovely veggie pulp sandwich with fresh veggie juices in a variety of combinations. There were lentils and Dr. Joe's cornbread, steel cut oats with sliced apples and pears with a little banana, goji berries, raisins, pea protein and psyllium husk. I have to admit, I pigged out.

The food they serve is spiritual, a ritual. It is an offering. It is sacred, like the vessel it enters. I certainly want to live a long healthy life. MAMA Naasira and Dr. Joe are scientists in this field. I am certainly consulting them (smile).

Thanks so much for the food.

Peace and Blessings,

–Wanda Sabir, San Francisco Bay Area

CHAPTER 4
Storage Containers

PREPARING FOOD FOR THE week requires that some food needs to be stored. Below are examples containers it which to store your food. As, mentioned above, pace yourself in obtaining food containers. Some of your are all ready set. You may have your food containers. But, for those of your who do not have food containers, you do not have to get everything at once.

Glass Food Containers
The best container for storing surplus food and keeping it healthy is made of glass, ceramic, and stainless steel. Use glass that is 100 percent recyclable and sustainable, safe and environmentally friendly, microwave safe, dishwater and freezer safe. The best glass containers have clips that lock to make the container airtight and measuring lines for visually monitoring intake.

Some glass containers have metal lids that contain Bisphenol A (BPA). BPA is a man-made chemical produced in large quantities for use primarily in the production of polycarbonate plastics (baby and water bottles, CDs, DVDs, sports equipment, lining water pipes) and epoxy resins.

Epoxy resins containing BPA are used to coat the inside of many metal products, such as bottle tops and lining food can. BPA is used in thermal paper used in sales receipts, and water supply lines. Some dental sealants and composites may contain BPA.

BPA is an endocrine disruptor. Endocrine disruptors are chemicals that may interfere with the body's endocrine system. The endocrine system is instrumental in regulating growth and development, tissue function, mood, metabolism, and fertility. The glands of the endocrine system and the hormones they release influence almost every cell, organ, and function of our bodies.

As the body's chemical messengers, hormones transfer information and instructions from one set of cells to another. BPA interferes with this function and may produce adverse developmental, reproductive, and immune effects in our bodies. Research shows that endocrine disruptors, like BPA, may pose the greatest risk during prenatal and early postnatal development when organ and neural systems are forming.

BPA can seep into food or beverages from containers made with BPA. An example would be a rusted metal lid of a glass bottle or jar that contains epoxy resin used to coat the inside of the metal. Exposure to BPA is a concern because of the possible health effects. The FDA has banned BPA from baby bottles, Sippy cups, and infant formula packaging. The European Union and Canada have banned BPA use in baby bottles.

Glass and BPA free lids are safer for you and your food. The best containers are airtight. If you do not have glass containers save your glass jars. Thoroughly wash the jars and lids. Dry them and used them as food containers until you can do better. Glass may be a challenge because it is subject to breaking. But, it is a preferable alternative to plastics that can harm you and the environment.

"Bisphenol A" http://bit.ly/1LVzpoY
"Best Food Storage Containers" http://exm.nr/1Mtk6LY
"BPA" http://mayocl.in/1SdTQtN
"Endocrine Disruptors" http://1.usa.gov/1Ioouf8
"Endocrine System" http://bit.ly/1IpGvUb

Stainless Steel Food Containers

Stainless Steel (SS) is non-toxic and lighter than glass. These food containers are stainless and do not promote a hospitable environment for the growth of bacteria. SS will not transfer odors or leave noticeable stains like tomato sauce, which are common complaints of plastic containers. SS containers are airtight, leak-proof, durable, and long lasting. But, visually, you can't view the contents in SS containers unless you open the top of the container.

While stainless steel may scratch, it will always look clean if it is well cleaned. SS may dent if dropped on a hard surface, but it will not chip or break like glass, or crack like plastic containers. These containers do not can go into the microwave.

SS does not chemically react to acidic foods (such as tomatoes) when cooking. Although light-weight aluminum and copper metals conduct heat extremely well, these metals impart a metallic taste and discolor light-colored sauces and soups. Not so with stainless steel. But, it is not recommended to store highly acidic foods in stainless steel containers.

Stainless steel is highly recyclable. SS contains iron, nickel, and chromium that can be harmful to your health. Once a stainless steel container has been scratched, even through normal scouring, the leaching of metals is higher. Look for high quality, heavy-duty stainless steel containers.

Stainless Steel containers can cost two or three times more than comparable plastic ones. Given how hygienic, stain-resistant, and unbreakable they are, they will outlast your plastic containers. They are safe enough to pass them down to your children.

Advantages of Stainless Steel Food Storage Containers"
http://bit.ly/1IooMTl
"What Are the Benefits of Quality Food Storage Containers"
http://bit.ly/1D7cJYD
"How Safe is Your Cookware" http://bit.ly/1I8sLxT

Ceramic

Ceramic containers are more versatile in its use than glass or stainless steel containers. These containers have an attractive appearance. The surface needs no polishing and does not corrode. Scouring powder can be used on ceramics without scarring the high-gloss coating. Unlike cast iron and other metallic pots and pans, it does not require seasoning to perform well.

Ceramic containers can be used with no trace metals leeching into your food. They can put up with direct heat from a stove burner, tolerate heat from home or commercial-grade ovens, and can store leftover food in both refrigerator and freezer. Ceramic containers retain heat very well and can keep your food hot longer than your typical serving containers can.

Ceramics containers can be warmed in the microwave. They can be put in the dishwasher. You can use any utensils you please with ceramic containers without chemical reactions. Be aware, antique ceramic may contain lead. It is better to buy it new.

"As of this writing a recommended ceramic cookware product is the Mercola Healthy Cookware" www.mercola.com

"Benefits of Cooking With Ceramics" http://amzn.to/1eyiClD

Plastic Containers

Plastics contain chemicals such as BPA, PVC, and phthalates that can leech into the food. Polyvinyl chloride (PVC) is the third most widely produced plastic, after polyethylene and polypropylene. It is used in construction replacing copper, iron, or wood in some areas. PVC can be made soft and more flexible by the addition of plasticizers (substances added to plastics to increase their flexibility, transparency, durability, and longevity) like phthalates. Phthalates are industrial chemicals used primary to soften PVC. Phthalates can cause liver, kidney, and organ damage.

Plastic containers become warped when used for a long period of time. This prevents tight sealing. This creates a health risk. Foods refrigerated in containers that are not airtight and tightly sealed allow oxygen to enter. A faint appearance and bad odor can develop. This is due to bacteria contamination and molds. Proper sealing prevents oxygen entrance. This reduces the moisture around the refrigerated food creating an unsuitable environment for bacteria. To prevent food decay, dry goods getting stale, and food poisoning store your food in airtight and properly sealed containers.

Avoid heat with plastic containers. Do not microwave, put in dishwasher, or store hot food in polycarbonate plastics. The National Institute of Environmental Health Sciences, part of the National Institute of Heath advises against this practice. That is because the plastic may break down over time and allow BPA to leach into food. Scratches inside your container can harbor bacteria even after washing. Use quality durable containers for securing your food for a longer period and protecting you from food contamination.

"Endocrine Disruptors" http://1.usa.gov/1I00uf8

Plastic Bags

At all temperatures plastic leaches some chemicals into food. If you buy food in bulk, or fresh vegetables, do not keep it in the thin plastic shopping bags you carry your food home in. These plastic bags as well as plastic shrink-wrap, are made of a plastic called low density polyethylene (LDP). LDP causes phthalic acid to be released to travel to your otherwise healthy food. That can cause liver damage, fertility problems, and hormonal imbalance.

CHAPTER 5
Basic Kitchen Safety Tips

Cooking is life sustaining, creative and fun, but disasters can occur in the kitchen. There are knives that cut fingers, bacteria that cause disease, fires that burn people and houses, glass that breaks and cuts, electrical shocks, water that scalds, and slips and falls from spills. To avert unpleasant cooking experiences, these tips are good to remember.

Wash your hands in hot, soapy water before cooking. We recommend healthy, environmentally friendly hand soaps.

Pay attention or focus on what you're doing in the kitchen.

Immediately clean up any spill. Wet floors are dangerously slippery.

Never leave children unsupervised in the kitchen. All knives, ovens, hot liquids, hot pots of food and electrical appliances present a potential danger.

Do not wear loose sleeves or sweaters while cooking. They can catch on to handles of pots on the range or stove. Wearing an apron also will protect your clothes.

Do not leave food unattended while cooking on top of the stove or range. Cut off each burner on the stove or range as you finish cooking each dish. If you have food in the oven and you must go into another area, set and take your timer with you.

Always turn pot and skillet handles away from the front of the stove, toward the back of the range or stove so they cannot be reached by children or accidentally pulled off the stove as you walk by.

Use one or more timers in the kitchen. This alerts you when food is cooked and helps avoid overcooking and starting fires.

When handling knives:

(a) Always cut away from your body.

(b) Always use a chopping or cutting board.

(c) Keep knives sharpened. A dull knife is more dangerous than a sharp one. The pressure you use to cut with a dull knife can cause it to slip, resulting in injury. Also, a cut with a dull knife is not a straight one.

(d) Do not place knives in a sink of soapy water. They may not be seen and injury can occur.

(e) When washing and drying knives, always keep the sharp edge away from your hands.

(f) Do not place knives in drawers with other utensils. This can result in injury.

(g) Store knives in a wooden block or in a separate section of a drawer.

(h) Keep knives out of the reach of children.

(i) Do not attempt to catch a knife if it falls. It is better for it to hit the floor than cut your hand.

10. Scalding can occur from hot steam. Be careful when opening hot ovens or lifting lids from hot food. Move your head away from hot steam before viewing the food.

11. If you are cooking in two or more pots on top of the stove or range at the same time, when the dish next to those still cooking is done, take it off the stove or range. The heat coming from those dishes still cooking can overcook the done dish, resulting in less nutrition and diminished flavors.

12. Keep paper towels, potholders, oven mitts and dishtowels nearby. Use them, but be careful to keep them away from an open flame or heated electrical range.

13. Keep salt, flour or baking soda close in case of a grease fire. Douse it with one of these if you do not have a fire extinguisher. Never pour water on a grease fire; it will only spread.

14. Be sure all appliances such as mixers, blenders, and can openers are unplugged before touching their sharp edges. Also, check carefully to be sure no utensil is left in an electrical device before it is turned on. Never stick a fork or knife into a toaster when it is plugged in.

15. Do not add water to a pan containing hot oil. It could make the oil spatter and cause injury.

16. Turn the oven off and unplug all cooking devices before you leave the kitchen.

"Basic Rules of Kitchen Safety"
http://bit.ly/1Bx4zb0
"Safety Tips in the Kitchen"
http://bit.ly/1dZv5ij
"28 Basic Kitchen Safety Tips"
http://bit.ly/1GiyNva
"Basic Rules of Kitchen Safety"
http://bit.ly/1Bx4zb0

CHAPTER 6
Naasira's Approach

A SUSTAINABLE PLAN FOR FOOD PREPARATION

OPTIMUM HEALTH IS A desire for many of us and we know that proper nutrition, healthy lifestyles, and a good diet are essential to this quest. There are many approaches to healthy eating, just as there are many former vegans and vegetarians. Some have abandoned the vegan or vegetarian diet because they no longer wished to cook or prepare food. A lack of a sustainable approach to weekly vegan or vegetarian cooking has been the main reason. We invite you to try Naasira's approach, as she has used it to create optimum health for herself and others and is now sharing it with you. This will require setting aside time to prepare and cook for the week. This will turn out to be one of the best times in your life.

To start off, we need to stock our kitchen. Below is a working list of the fruits, vegetables, spices, herbs, breads, flours, spreads and nut butters, seasonings, oils, sweeteners, plant–based milks such as almond or hemp milk, beans, grains, super–foods, and snacks we will use.

I would not suggest getting everything at once. Obtain the items required for each recipe you are working on. I would suggest listing all the recommended items for your kitchen. Pick up a few non–perishable items such as rice, beans, nuts, or grains on the list each time you go to the market, farmer, or store.

Fruits and vegetables are best eaten fresh. Only purchase the fruits and vegetables you will eat during the week. This keeps the fruits and vegetable fresh. They contain more minerals, vitamins, and healthy fruit fiber. Always remember, fresh is best.

Your stocked kitchen will provide you flexibility, options, and creativity. You can also think of your kitchen as your health science laboratory. Here, you will assemble herbs, spices, fruits, grains, and vegetables to give your body food to aid in its optimal repair and healing. Make sure you put your food in safe containers. This will protect your food against spoilage and not expose your food to unhealthy substances.

Stock Your Kitchen

Organic, non-genetically modified organisms (GMO), non-pesticide sprayed foods are best. But if they are not available, use Grocery/Health Food Stores/Online.

- **Beans**
  - Adzuki beans
  - Black beans
  - Black-eyed peas
  - Chickpeas (garbanzo beans)
  - Lentils (French, green, red, black)
  - Navy beans
  - Red Kidney beans
  - Split peas
  - Any other type of bean you like
- **Breads/Flour/Pasta**
  - Spouted-grain bread(raisin, cinnamon, or sesame)
  - Whole-grain pita bread
  - Barley Flour
  - Brown Rice Flour
  - Buckwheat Flour
  - Quinoa Flour
  - Rye Flour
- **Condiments**
  - Black sesame seeds

- Catsup
- Mustard
- Pickles
- **Dried Fruit**
- Apricots
- Figs
- Goji Berries
- Medjool dates
- Mulberries
- Prunes
- Raisins
- **Herbs And Spices**
- Allspice (whole, powder)
- Basil
- Bay leaf
- Black Pepper
- Cardamon (seed, powder)
- Cayenne
- Cinnamon powder
- Cinnamon sticks
- Chipotle
- Cloves (whole, powder)
- Coriander (seed, powder)
- Cumin (seed, powder)
- Curry
- Dill (seed, powder)
- Fennel (seed, powder)
- Fenugreek (seed, powder)
- Herbes de Provence
- Italian
- Mineral salt
- Nutmeg (whole, powder)
- Nutritional yeast
- Marjoram

- Oregano
- Paprika
- Rosemary
- Sage
- Sea salt
- Sumac
- Thyme
- Turmeric
- Vegan bouillon cubes
- **Fresh fruit** (seasonal purchases are best)
- Apples
- Avocados
- Bananas
- Blueberries
- Cherries
- Cucumbers
- Figs
- Grapes
- Kiwi
- Mangoes
- Oranges
- Papayas
- Peaches
- Pears
- Persimmons
- Plantain
- Strawberries
- Tomatoes (including cherry)
- Watermelon
- Or any other fruit you like.
- **Fresh Herbs**
- Basil
- Dill
- Fennel

- Ginger
- Rosemary
- Thyme
- **Fresh Vegetables** (seasonal purchases are best)
- Arugula
- Asparagus
- Basil
- Beets
- Beet Greens
- Bell Peppers (green/red/yellow)
- Bitter Melon
- Broccoli
- Cabbage (red, Napa, green)
- Cauliflower
- Carrots
- Celery
- Cilantro
- Collard Greens
- Dandelion Greens
- Dill
- Eggplant
- Fennel
- Ginger
- Kale
- Leeks
- Mushrooms
- Mustard Greens
- Peas
- Parsley
- Peppers (hot)
- Rosemary
- Shallots
- Scallions
- Spinach

- String Beans
- Swiss Chard
- Thyme
- Turnip Greens
- Sweet potatoes
- Yams
- **Frozen Fruit** (freeze it in season)
- Bananas
- Blackberries
- Blueberries
- Cherries
- Raspberries
- Strawberries
- **Grains**
- Barley (hulled)
- Couscous
- Millet
- Polenta
- Quinoa
- Black, Wild, Red, Jasmine or Brown Basmati Rice
- Rolled Oats
- Steel Cut Oats
- **Liquid Seasoning**
- Bragg Liquid Aminos
- Shoyu
- **Nuts/Seeds**
- Almonds
- Cardamom seeds
- Caraway seeds
- Cashews
- Chia seeds
- Coriander seeds
- Flax seeds
- Hemp seeds

- Pine nuts
- Pistachios
- Pumpkin seeds
- Sesame seeds
- Sunflower seeds
- Walnuts
- **Oils**
- Extra Virgin olive oil
- Virgin Coconut oil
- Flaxseed oil
- Omega Twin
- **Plant–Based Milks**
- Almond milk
- Coconut milk
- Hemp Non–Dairy Beverage
- Hemp milk
- **Spreads and Butters**
- Almond butter, raw
- Cashew butter, raw
- Miso (made from fermented soybeans and salt) red or white
- Organic Raw Black Sesame Tahini
- Tahini butter
- **Snacks**
- Non–dairy, non–soy yogurt
- Popcorn
- Plantain
- **Sweeteners**
- Black Strap Molasses
- Maple Syrup
- Coconut Nectar
- **Superfood**s
- Maca
- Protein power

- Psyllium husk
- Moringa
- Pea Protein

The goal of this method is to ensure you have fresh, healthy food readily available so you will not resort to unhealthy food choices. A well stocked kitchen will serve you well in your new, healthy eating lifestyle. When preparing food for the week, keep in mind the goal. The items you purchase or select will be for cornbread, stir-fry (sauté), salad, smoothies, juices, and African vegetable stew. The collard green wraps, spaghetti sauce, tacos, Sloppy Joes, pizzas, lasagna, and other dishes are spin-offs of the African vegetable stew.

Farmers' Markets

Most of your fresh fruit, nuts, olive oil, and vegetables may be purchased at the Farmers' Market. Here are some helpful tips.

The farmers can give you lots of information about the items you purchase, like the health benefits, the different varieties and ways to prepare the produce.

If you are a regular customer, most farmers will charge you less. Once farmers get to know you, they generally will look out for you. This can be in the form of saving goods for you, letting you know when certain foods are in season, or bringing goods for you.

There is generally a discount on the goods sold near closing time. That is because the farmers would rather sell the goods at a lower price or give them away to avoid having to pack them up to take back to the farm or warehouse only to be packed up and sold another day. Also, the goods might be too ripe to sell another day.

There are a few disadvantages of coming to the Farmers' Market near closing. The best looking fruits and vegetables are usually sold early in the day, so by the time you arrive, what's left may have been picked over and not look so pretty. But once it is washed, chopped, and cut up for salads, stews, roasted vegetables or stir-fry, the initial look of the produce will not matter.

Grocery/Health Food Stores/Online

The items that cannot be obtained from the Farmers' Market usually can be found at the grocery or health food store. Many large groceries have a health food or organic food section. Most health food stores will have some of the items listed above. Many of these items may also be purchased online.

Now, some of you may hesitate when you discover organic or non-pesticide sprayed, non-GMO fruits and vegetables cost more than conventional fruits and vegetables. But I invite you to compare the price of the average medical bills you receive for treatment because of the damage caused by pesticides and waxes from conventionally grown fruits and vegetables to the price paid for organic or non-pesticide sprayed , non-GMO fruits and vegetables. Your body will appreciate the healthy choice.

The Food Industries are motivated by profit. If there is a demand and a profit can be made selling organic or non-pesticide sprayed, non-GMO food, the food industries will find a way to make it available to the consumers. As more people voice their demand for organic, non-pesticide sprayed, non-GMO foods, the food industries will comply. This will create more competition between competing food companies. This results in prices in stores being lowered as more companies rise to meet the consumer's demands.

There are growing numbers of people who desire a healthier way of eating. This includes, the "hipsters" and "baby-boomers" that have considerable economic influence. Talk to your local store managers. Tell them that you want them to obtain organic or non-pesticide sprayed, non-GMO fruits and vegetables.

CHAPTER 7
Recipes

Spicy African Stew

THIS AMOUNT OF STEW is designed to last for 5 days. The stew is the foundation for the salad, pizza, Sloppy Joes, eggplant casserole, lasagna and other recipes. The vegetables are soaked, rinsed, and cut up. The salad is put together in a large bowl from the cut up vegetables. The salad is then covered and refrigerated before the cooking of the stew. Most of the vegetables left after making the salad are put in the stew.

Keep in mind the vegetables listed are based on the season. All the vegetables listed may not be available. Other vegetables that are in season or available may be substituted. If there are any vegetables left that are not used in the salad or stew, cover and store them in the refrigerator for use in other recipes. Add more spices to the stew each day before reheating the portion of the stew to be eaten that day. This adds more flavor and taste.

Cook time about 1 hour Serves 8–12

Large Pot (8 Quarts)
To make the paste or rue, heat the pot on low.
Add: 2–3 tablespoons Oil (Coconut or Olive)

Increase heat to medium low, then sauté these seeds in the oil for 6–8 minutes:

1 ½ tablespoons Fennel Seeds

2 tablespoons Cumin Seeds

1½ tablespoons Coriander Seeds. Increase heat to medium.

Add: 1 cup scallions (chopped) Sauté scallions with seeds until brown.

Add:

2 Tomatoes (medium sized). Lower heat to medium low

1 can Tomato Paste (6 oz)

2 Vegetable Bouillon Cubes

Add: 1 cup chopped Leeks

½ cup Shallots

½ cup Ginger

2 Bay Leaves (medium sized)

2 tablespoons Oil (Coconut or Olive)

Add: 2 cups of vegetable stems from collards, broccoli, kale, beet, and cauliflower. Stir occasionally to avoid sticking to bottom of pot for 4–6 minutes. Add:

1 quart Vegetable Broth

1 Cinnamon Stick

1 teaspoon Thyme

1 teaspoon Rosemary

2 tablespoons Ground Cumin

2 tablespoons Ground Coriander

2 tablespoons Turmeric

Optional Dry Spices:

1 teaspoon Paprika

1 teaspoon Sage

½ teaspoon Marjoram

½ teaspoon Fenugreek

1 can Coconut Milk (13.5 oz)

1 tablespoon Almond Butter

½ cup Beans (Soak beans overnight or at least: 1 hour for Lentils, 2–4 hours, for Mung, Adzuki, Red, Kidney or Black Beans)
1 cup Water
1 cup Yellow Squash/Zucchini
Place lid on pot. Boil 10–15 minutes on medium high heat. Stir occasionally.
Add: 1 Glass jar – Organic Salsa (12oz)
Cover pot with lid. Turn heat low for 10 minutes.
2 tablespoons Oregano
1 tablespoon Chipotle
1 teaspoon Ground Basil

> *Optional*
> 1 tablespoon Dried Seaweed
> ½ teaspoon Sumac
> ½ teaspoon Jalapeño Peppers

½ teaspoon Mineral Salt
¼ teaspoon Cayenne Pepper
1½ tablespoons Bragg Liquid Aminos
2 tablespoons Chickpea Miso Non–Soy, Non–GMO
1 tablespoon Maple Syrup
1 cup chopped Beets
Continue to stir for 4–6 minutes on medium heat. Then
Add: 1 Vegetable Bouillon Cube
1 cup thinly sliced Potatoes (Purple, Red, Yukon)
Place lid on pot. Stir occasionally 5–8 minutes: Add chopped:
1 cup Fresh Basil
1 cup Bok Choy (seasonal)
1 cups Daikon
1 cup Celery
1 cup Green or Red Bell Pepper
1 cup Cauliflower
1 cup Beets Greens

1 cup chopped Fennel

Optional Vegetables:

½ cup Dill Weed

1 cup Dandelion

1 cup Carrots

½ cup Spearmint

1 cup Water if needed (if you desirer a thicker stew, use less water)

Place lid on the pot for 10–15 minutes. Stir occasionally. **Add:**

2 cups Cabbage

2 cups Collard Greens

1 cup Parsley

3 cups Kale (Curly or Dinosaur)

1 cup Broccoli

Optional Vegetables:

2 cups Green Beans

1 cup chopped Asparagus

½ cup Cilantro

Cover pot with lid. Turn heat low for 10 minutes.

Almond Arugula Pesto

Prep Time: 15 minutes   Makes 1½ –2 Cups

Ingredients:

¾ teaspoon Mineral or Sea Salt

1 tablespoon chopped Shallots

3 bunches Arugula or Basil Leaves (no stems)

¾ cup Coconut or Olive oil

1 teaspoon Turmeric

1 teaspoon Omega or Flax Oil

1½ tablespoon Lemon Juice

2 tablespoons Whole Almonds

½ cup Hemp Seeds

3 tablespoons Nutritional Yeast

¼ teaspoon Cayenne

Optional:

1 tablespoon Pine Nuts

Directions:

Place all ingredients except for hemp seeds and almonds in a food processor fitted with the "S" blade. Pulse and scrape down the sides of the bowl until smooth. While processor is running add the almonds and hemp seeds. Pulse until desired smoothness. Eat immediately or store in airtight container in the refrigerator.

Almond Coconut Date Rolls

Prep Time: 15 minutes
Blend Time: 2–3 minutes   Makes 10–12 Rolls

Ingredients:
1 cup pitted Dates
1 cup raw Ground Almonds
1 pinch of Mineral or Sea Salt
¼ cup shredded unsweetened dried Coconut
½ teaspoon Cinnamon
½ teaspoon Cardamom
1 tablespoon Coconut Oil

Blending Instructions:

Blend cardamom, cinnamon, almonds, oil, salt, dates and coconut in a blender or food processor 2–3 minutes until it becomes a paste. Roll tablespoonfuls of the paste into 1–2 inch balls.

Eat, refrigerate, or freeze until later. Enjoy!

Optional: Sprinkle coconut on top of rolls.

Almond Banana Smoothie

Prep Time: 15 minutes   **Makes 4–6 Cups**

Ingredients:

Nuts: ¼ cup Almonds: Soak almonds overnight or 8 hours or longer. If there is a time crunch, soak almonds for at least 2 hours. Rinse and drain almonds and place them in the blender.

Dry Ingredients:

1 tablespoon Flax seed
1 tablespoon Chia Seed
1 tablespoons Maca
½ teaspoon Chlorella
2 pitted Medjool Dates
1 teaspoon Cinnamon

Optional:

½ teaspoon Spirulina
½ teaspoon Iris Moss
½ teaspoon Psyllium Husk
1 teaspoon Hemp Seeds
2 Prunes
¼ cup Walnuts, Sunflower, Pumpkin Seeds

Liquids:

1/2 cup Hemp Milk
½ cup Water
1 cup Ice
½ cup Coconut Water
1 teaspoon Omega Twin

Optional:

1 teaspoon Aloe Vera Gel
½ cup Apple Juice

Fruit:

2 Banana
¼ cup chopped Pineapples
½ Apple
¼ cup Blueberries

Optional

¼ cup Strawberries
1/4 cup Kale

Directions:
Pour all ingredients into Blender for 2–3 minutes.
Serve immediately or refrigerate. Enjoy!

Almond Milk

Prep Time: 10 minutes
Makes 3 ½ Cups
Ingredients:
Nut milk bag or Cheesecloth
1 cup Raw Almonds
3½ cups Water
3–4 pitted Medjool Dates
½ teaspoon powdered Vanilla
½ teaspoon Cardamom
½ teaspoon Cinnamon
1/8 teaspoon of Mineral or Sea Salt
Optional:
1 tablespoon Raw Cacao
½ teaspoon Allspice
½ teaspoon Nutmeg
½ teaspoon Iris Moss

Directions: Soak almonds overnight or 8 hours or longer. If there is a time crunch, soak almonds for at least 2 hours. Rinse and drain almonds and place them in the blender. Add water, dates and vanilla. Blend on high speed for 2 minutes or until smooth. Place a nut milk bag or cheesecloth over a large bowl. Pour the milk mixture into the bag or strain through cheesecloth.

Gently, squeeze the bottom of the milk bag or squeeze milk from cheesecloth. This may take 3–4 minutes. Rinse out the blender and pour the milk back into the blender. Add cinnamon, cardamom and salt. Blend on low for 30 seconds. Serve immediately or refrigerate in an airtight glass jar container for up to 3–5 days.

Baked Butternut Squash

Prep Time: 10 min.
Cooking Time: 1 hour
9x13 Baking dish
Serves 6–8
Ingredients:

2 Butternut Squash
½ cup Water
1½ Vegetable Bouillon cube
1 tablespoon chopped Ginger
1 teaspoon Maple syrup
1 tablespoon chopped Shallots
2 tablespoons Oil (Coconut or Olive)
1 tablespoon chopped Scallions
¼ cup Parsley
Mineral or Sea Salt to taste
1 tablespoon Bragg Liquid Aminos
1 tablespoon ground Basil
1 tablespoon ground Thyme
1 teaspoon Chipotle

Optional:
1 teaspoon Rosemary
1 teaspoon Fennel
1 teaspoon Coriander
1 teaspoon Turmeric

Directions: Preheat oven to 400 Fahrenheit (204 Celsius). Rinse off each squash. Cut each squash into halves. Place each half in a large baking dish flesh side up. Put ½ tablespoon Oil in the middle of each squash. Sprinkle herbs and seasoning on the halves to taste. Cover pan and bake 45–60 minutes or until skin is tender and easily pierced with a fork. Eat. Enjoy!

Baked French Fries

Prep Time: 15 minutes
Cook Time 25–30 minutes
Serves 2–4
Ingredients:

6 Yukon potatoes

3 Sweet potatoes

½ cup Coconut or Olive Oil

1 tablespoon medium chopped Shallots

1 teaspoon Allspice

1 teaspoon Sumac

1 teaspoon Turmeric

1 teaspoon Cayenne Pepper

1 teaspoon Paprika

1 teaspoon Mineral Salt

1 teaspoon Italian Seasoning

Directions:

Preheat oven to 400 Fahrenheit (204 Celsius).

Wash potatoes. Leave as much skin on the potatoes as possible. Cut potatoes into French fry slices. Place potatoes in oiled pan. Sprinkle spices evenly on potatoes. Massage potatoes with oil and spices. Place the pan of potatoes into the oven at 400 degrees Fahrenheit (204 Celsius) for 25–35 minutes.

Remove cooked potatoes from oven and place on plate. Eat. Enjoy!

Banana Fruit Cookies

Makes 36–40 Cookies
Cook Time: 10–15 Minutes
Dry Ingredients:
½ cup Barley Flour
½ cup Quinoa Flour
½ cup Buckwheat Flour
½ cup Rolled Oats
2 tablespoons Baking Powder
½ teaspoon Anise Powder
½ teaspoon Baking Soda
1½ teaspoon Vanilla Powder
1 teaspoon Mace powder
1 teaspoon Clove Powder
1 teaspoon Nutmeg Powder
1 tablespoon Cinnamon Powder
1 teaspoon Allspice
1 teaspoon Mineral or Sea Salt
2 tablespoons Flax Seeds
2 teaspoons Dry Yeast (1 packet)
¼ cup Raisins

Optional
¼ cup pitted dried Dates
¼ cup chopped Walnuts
1 teaspoon Ginger Powder
¼ cup Pineapple
¼ cup Strawberries
¼ cup Coconut chips

Wet Ingredients:
4 Bananas (ripe)
1 cup Water
¼ cup Orange Peel
½ cup grated Carrots
¼ cup Blueberries

Optional
¼ cup chopped Prunes
¼ cup Oil (Coconut or Olive)
¼ cup chopped Apples
1 cup Coconut Milk
1 cup water

Instructions:
In a small bowl warm the 1 cup of water
Add a drop of maple syrup in the water and stir

Mix in the active yeast

Keep in warm place for the yeast to froth for 10 minutes

Combine flour, oatmeal, baking soda and powder, vanilla, mace, cloves, nutmeg, cinnamon, allspice, mineral or sea salt, flax seeds into a large bowl. Grade carrots and orange peel and add chopped apples, bananas, raisins, blueberries, prunes, oil, maple syrup, into another large bowl. Spoon flour into bowl with the fruits and add water and coconut milk stirring or blending everything together.

Preheat oven to 325 Fahrenheit (162 Celsius). Grease baking sheet really well and sprinkle a little flour on it to prevent cookies from sticking to baking sheet. Drop in 2 tablespoon sized mounds on baking sheet. Allow cookies to bake 10–15 minutes or until edges are barely golden brown.

Temperatures may vary. The gas oven may need to bake 5 minutes longer than an electric oven. Cookies may bake up to 20 minutes and it does not matter if they are a little dark. Remove cookies from oven. Allow them to cool for 10–12 minutes. Use spatula to remove cookies from baking sheet

Banana Fruit Loaf

Makes 2–3 loaves
Cook Time: 2 Hours 10 Minutes
Dry Ingredients:
½ cup Barley Flour
½ cup Quinoa Flour

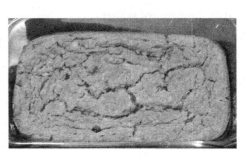

½ cup Buckwheat Flour
½ cup Rolled Oats
2 tablespoons Baking Powder
½ teaspoon Baking Soda
1½ teaspoon Vanilla Powder
1 teaspoon Mace Powder
1 teaspoon Clove Powder
1 teaspoon Nutmeg Powder
1 tablespoon Cinnamon Powder
1 teaspoon Allspice
1 teaspoon Mineral or Sea Salt
2 tablespoons Flax Seeds
2 teaspoons Dry Yeast (1 packet)
¼ cup chopped Prunes
¼ cup Raisins

Optional:
¼ cup pitted dried Dates
¼ cup chopped Walnuts
½ teaspoon Anise Powder
1 teaspoon Ginger Powder
¼ cup Pineapple
¼ cup Strawberries
¼ cup Coconut chips

Wet Ingredients:
4 bananas (ripe)
¼ cup Orange Peel
¼ cup chopped Apples
½ cup grated Carrots
¼ cup Blueberries
Preheat oven to 325 Fahrenheit (162 Celsius).

Instructions:

In a small bowl
Warm the 1 cup of water
Add a drop of maple syrup in the water and stir
Mix in the active yeast
Keep in warm place for the yeast to froth for 10 minutes

Combine flour, oatmeal, baking soda and powder, vanilla, mace, cloves, nutmeg, cinnamon, allspice, mineral or sea salt, flax seeds into a large bowl. Grade carrots and orange peel and add chopped apples, raisins, blueberries, prunes, oil, maple syrup, into another large bowl. Add a couple of spoons of flour into bowl with the fruits and add water and coconut milk stirring everything together.

Grease 2 to 3 bread pans really well and sprinkle a little flour on greased pans to prevent fruit bread from sticking to pans. Allow bread to bake 2 hours and 10 minutes. Check loaf with toothpick by inserting it in the middle and remove. If done there should be a few moist crumbs attached, but not batter.

Temperatures may vary. The gas oven may bake 20 minutes longer than an electric oven. The bread may bake over 2 hours and 30 minutes, and it does not matter if it is a little dark. Remove bread from oven. Allow loaves to cool 1 hour. Use spatula to remove fruit bread from pan.

Blueberry Almond Butter Smoothie

Prep time: 5 minutes
Makes 1 large Smoothie
Ingredients:
1 cup frozen Blueberries
1 cup frozen Banana
½ cup Almond Milk
1 heaping tablespoon Almond Butter
½ teaspoon Vanilla Powder
1 teaspoon Maple Syrup or to taste
1 cup Water

Directions:
Combine all ingredients into a blender. Blend until smooth. Drink! Enjoy!

Optional:
½ cup Strawberries
½ teaspoon Cinnamon

Wild Rice

Serves 6–8

Cooking Time: 45 minutes

Wild rice is not really rice, but a delicious member of the grass family. It is a native of North America and is traditionally grown (wild) in river beds and isolated lake locations. It holds its long shape with cooking and retains a nutty texture.

Wild rice contains twice as much protein as brown rice. It is rich in antioxidants, containing up to 30 times more than white rice. Wild rice is a good source of essential minerals and vitamins A, C and E. It can be eaten by diabetics, since it is lower in carbohydrates and calories and higher in fiber than rice.

Ingredients:

1 cup Wild Rice

2 cups Water

1/4 teaspoon Mineral or Sea Salt

1/4 teaspoon ground Cumin

1 teaspoon Turmeric

1/2 teaspoon Paprika

1/4 teaspoon Coriander

1/4 teaspoon Basil

1/4 teaspoon Cloves

Optional:

1/4 teaspoon Saffron

3 Cardamom Seeds

Directions:

Boil 2 cups of water adding salt, Cumin, Turmeric, Paprika, Coriander and Basil for 3-5 minutes. Pour in Rice and stir. Turn heat to low, cover and let rice simmer 25-30 minutes, stirring occasionally to avoid burning the bottom of the pot or pan. Remove from heat. Stir, leave uncovered 15-20 minutes to let the grains separate. Eat, enjoy!

Citrus Drink

Makes ¾–1 Gallon

Ingredients:
1 quart Water
2 quarts Apple Juice or Apple Cider
2 Oranges
1 Apple
2 Lemons
2 Limes
1 Grapefruit
1 tablespoon sliced Ginger
1 tablespoon chopped Shallots
¼ teaspoon Cayenne pepper
1 Cinnamon Stick
1 teaspoon Cinnamon Powder
2 whole Nutmeg
4–6 whole Allspice
4–6 whole Cloves
1 teaspoon Turmeric Powder
½ teaspoon Burdock Root

Optional:
¼ cup Scallions
1 teaspoon Dandelion Root

Directions:
Wash fruit
Slice fruit
Place sliced fruit in pot
Pour water and apple juice or apple cider in pot
Add ginger, shallots, cayenne pepper, cinnamon and turmeric powder.

Place cinnamon stick, whole nutmeg, whole allspice, whole coves, dandelion and burdock root in a muslin bag or cheesecloth mesh.

Place Muslin bag in the pot. Simmer on medium heat 1 hour with lid slightly jarred. The longer it simmers, the thicker the drink.

When drink is gone, you can refill pot with water, apple juice or cider and simmer for 25 minutes. Enjoy!

Cocoa Mousse

Total Time: Prep: 15 min. + 1 hour Chilling
Makes: 6 Servings
Ingredients:
1 ripe Avocado
1¼ cups Hemp or Almond Milk
1/3 cup Coconut Nectar or Maple Syrup
¼ cup Cocoa Powder
1 teaspoon Vanilla extract
Directions:

In a blender, combine milk, coconut nectar or Maple syrup, avocado, cocoa and vanilla. Puree until smooth and well combined.

Spoon mixture into glasses or serving bowls. Cover and chill in the refrigerator for at least 1 hour.

Eat, enjoy!

Collard Green Wraps

**There are 4 parts:
Spread Wraps,
African Stew or
Wrap Sauce,
Plant Protein Filling
Added ingredients.
Makes 10–12 wraps
Prep Time:** 40 minutes
Plant Protein Filling
Ingredients:
2 cups Raw Sunflower Seeds
5 oz Olives (Black, Green or Kalamata)
1 Cup chopped Shallots
¼ cup Lemon or Lime Juice
½ teaspoon Mineral or Sea Salt
1 teaspoon Turmeric
½ teaspoon ground Basil
1 tablespoon Sesame Seeds
½ cup chopped Scallions
1 tablespoon Cumin
2 tablespoons Cilantro
½ cup Beets
¼ teaspoon Cayenne Pepper
½ cup Bell Pepper
2 tablespoons Oil (Coconut or Olive)

Optional:
¼ teaspoon chopped Ginger Root
¼ cup chopped Celery
¼ teaspoon Chipole
2 tablespoons Tomato
2 tablespoons Parsley
½ cup Carrots
1 teaspoon Oregano

Add and place in four (4) separate bowls:
1 chopped Mango or Persimmon
1 sliced Avocado

1 chopped Cucumber (medium sized)

1 cubed or chopped Baked Yam or Sweet Potato (medium sized)

Directions:

In a food processor combine oil, salt, seeds, olives, vegetables and spices. Add lemon or lime juice and pulse until smooth but still slightly crumbly.

Spread Wraps

To rinse collards: place in a large bowl with water and teaspoon sea salt. This will rid the collards of critters that want to hold on to the succulent collards. Rinse again without the sea salt.

Blot dry with paper towel. With a sharp knife slice the thickest part of the vein or stem thinly. Slice from the larger part of the vein or stem toward the narrow end of the vein or stem of the collards.

Boil one gallon of water. Generously salt with mineral or sea salt.

Drop 4–5 leaves in the pot of boiled water about 2–5 seconds. Remove and place in a bowl of ice cold water. Spread out collards on paper towels and blot dry.

African Stew (2–3 cups) or Wrap Sauce

Add 2–3 cups of blended Africn Vegetable Stew or Wrap Sauce.

Wrap Sauce:

1 tablespoon Coconut or Olive Oil
¼ teaspoon Mineral or Sea Salt
¼ cup chopped Scallions
¼ cup chopped Shallots
½ teaspoon Oregano
1 teaspoon Turmeric
½ teaspoons dried Basil
2 cups Salsa (medium or mild)
½ teaspoon Thyme
1 teaspoon Maple Syrup
1 Vegetable Bouillon cube

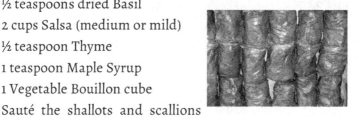

Sauté the shallots and scallions in oil for 1–2 minutes in a saucepan on medium heat. Add the other ingredients and stir. Reduce the heat to low and let it simmer, stirring occasionally for 5 –10 minutes. Remove from heat.

To Make Wrap:

Spread 1–2 teaspoons of blended "stew" or Wrap Sauce across collard leaf. Place 1–2 teaspoons of Plant Protein Filling on top. Feel free to add sliced avocado, yam or sweet potatoe, persimmon, mango and cucumber.

Roll the collards like you would a burrito. Cut in half and serve.

Optional sauce: Mix lemon juice, Shoyu, Tamari or Liquid Braggs Aminos, to taste. Drizzle over wraps or use for dipping.

Vegan Real Cornbread

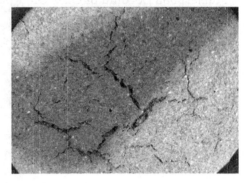

10 –12 servings
PrepTime: 10 minutes
Cook Tme: 35 minutes
Ingredients:
Dry:
1 tsp Baking Soda
¼ cup Polenta
1½ cups Cornmeal (blue or yellow)
1 cup flour (Quinoa, Buckwheat, Spelt, Rye, Amaranth, or Coconut)
½ teaspoon Mineral Salt or Sea Salt
2½ tablespoons Sesame Seeds
1½ tablespoon Flax Seeds
1½ tablespoon Baking powder (aluminum free)

Wet:
¼ – 1/3 cup Maple Syrup (to taste)
1/3 cup Olive Oil or Coconut Oil
1 cup Unsweetened Hemp or Almond Milk
1 cup water

Directions:
Preheat oven at 350°

Oil bottom of a large pan, large skillet, or Pyrex dish (9x13 inch). Sprinkle Sesame Seeds evenly on the oiled bottom. Mix dry and wet ingredients together in a large bowl. Pour mixed ingredients into pan, place in oven for 35 minutes. Remove from oven and allow to sit about 20 minutes. Be sure oven is off. (if cornbread is placed on top of the stove, it will continue to cook) Enjoy!

Daikon Kale Stir-Fry

Total Time: 23 min
Prep: 15 min
Cook: 8 min
Ingredients:

3 tablespoons Coconut or Olive Oil

¼ cup chopped Ginger — 1 teaspoon Turmeric

¼ cup chopped Shallots — ¼ teaspoon Mineral or Sea Salt

¾ cup chopped Scallions — 1 teaspoon Cumin

1 cup thinly sliced Bell Peppers — 1 teaspoon Oregano

½ cup shredded Daikon — 1 teaspoon Basil

¼ cup chopped Pineapple — 1 tablespoon Chipotle

2 bunches kale with leaves torn, stalks discarded, coarsely chopped.

Preparation Instructions:

Thoroughly soak kale in a large bowl with cold water with a dash of Sea Salt to remove grit and discourage little critters. Rinse off kale in cold water. Tear the leaves from the stalks, coarsely chop kale leaves.

Heat oil in a large skillet or wok over medium heat with bell pepper, daikon, scallions, shallots, ginger, salt, cumin, oregano, basil and chipotle. Stir it around 2–3 minutes so it won't burn.

Add kale and pineapple and stir around 3–5 minutes.

Remove cooked dish to a plate and serve!

Earthy Root Detox Tea

We suggest drinking one glass of water with a squeeze of lemon upon rising each day to aid your body moving out waste. To help in cleansing the body there seems to be nothing better than the roots of nature.

Ingredients:

1 Gallon Water
Chaparral
Patchouli
Shepherds Purse
Wild Yam
Oregon Grape
Yellow dock
Gota Kola
Dandelion
Red Clover
Cohosh
Bilberry
Licorice

Optional:
Lavender

Directions:

Place 1 teaspoon of each root in a Muslin bag or cheesecloth mesh in a large pot. Pour in 1 gallon of water over roots. Boil 40–45 minutes on medium high heat. Turn off heat and let steep for 1 hour. Drink immediately, reheat or refrigerate.

Be Healthy!

Egg Substitute

2 tablespoons corn starch = 1 egg
2 tablespoons arrowroot flour = 1 egg
1 tablespoons flax seeds + 1 cup water = 1 egg
1 banana or
¼ cup applesauce = 1 egg in baked goods such as pancakes, muffins or yeast-free quick breads, such as banana and pumpkin.

Fruit Grain Cereal

6–8 Servings –
Cooking Time:
25–30 minutes
Ingredients:
4 cups Water
¼ teaspoon Mineral or Sea Salt
½ teaspoon Mace
½ teaspoon Cloves
¼ cup Rolled Oats
1 teaspoon Turmeric
½ teaspoon Cardamom
½ teaspoon Cinnamon
½ teaspoon Nutmeg
1 tablespoon Coconut or Olive Oil
¼ cup Black Rice
¼ cup Red Rice
½ cup Quinoa
½ cup Steel Cut Oats
¼ cup Millet

Directions: Pour water into pan or pot. Add oil and spices and bring to boil 8–10 minutes. Adding Cinnamon Stick is optional. Pour in Grains. Reduce heat to low, cover and cook 15–20 minutes. Add Rolled Oats and stir. Cover for 3–5 minutes at low heat. Turn off heat and remove from burner. Remove lid. Stir and leave uncovered for 25–30 minutes to let the grains separate.

Place in large bowl:
¼ cup Blueberries
¼ cup Strawberry
¼ cup Banana
¼ Peach
¼ cup Apples
¼ cup Orange
¼ cup Mango
¼ cup Pineapple

Fruit is seasonal. If certain fruits are not available simply substitute other fruits. Mix fruit with desired amount of grains. Add Almond, Hemp Milk or Smoothie to taste.

Select from desired Power Boosters below and sprinkle to taste: raisins, dates, almonds, mulberries, goji berries, pates, hunza berries, hemp seeds, chia seeds, maca, spirulina, psyllium husk, moringa powder, Irish moss powder.

Refrigerate all fruit and grains that are not used for another day or other recipes.

Simple African Fufu

Prep Time: 10 minutes
Cook Time: 5 minutes
Serves: 2–4
Ingredients:
2 cups water
¼ teaspoon Mineral or Sea Salt
¾ or 1 cup Cassava Flour

Directions:
1. Boil two cups of water in a small pot or pan.
2. Remove boiling water from the burner.
3. Pour Cassava flour clockwise in the water.
4. Stir it slowly until it is thick enough to roll into a ball.
5. Dip or serve Fufu with soup or stew.

Enjoy!

Shallot Popcorn

Prep Time – 5 minutes –
Cook Time 2–3 minutes
Serves 2–4
Ingredients:
2 tablespoons Coconut or Olive oil
½ cup Popcorn
¼ teaspoon chopped Shallots

Directions:

Put the oil (Coconut or Olive) and chopped shallots in a large, deep pot or pan with a lid. Turn to medium–high heat. Add 2 kernels of popcorn, and cover.

Once the kernels pop, remove the cover and pour in the remaining popcorn. Cover and move pot or pan on top of heat in a circular motion, holding the cover on, until the popcorn is no longer popping. Remove popcorn from heat.

Optional:

Pour popcorn in a large bag. Sprinkle Mineral or Sea Salt, Cayenne pepper, Paprika, Cumin, Turmeric and/or Nutritional Yeast into the bag with the popcorn. Close the top of the bag. Shake bag of popcorn with the ingredients for about 5 –10 seconds. Eat popcorn. Enjoy!

Tasty Guacamole

Prep Time: 20
Makes 1 Batch
Ingredients:
3 ripe Avocados
1 cup Tomato
½ teaspoon Cumin
½ teaspoon Mineral or Sea Salt
½ Jalapeno Pepper (medium) minced
½ cup chopped Cilantro
½ teaspoon Cayenne
¼ chopped Shallots
1 tablespoon Lemon Juice

Optional:
¼ cup Bell Pepper

Directions:

Cut avocados in half and remove the seed. Scoop out flesh and place it in the blender. If you do not have a blender, place all ingredients in a large bowl and mix well. If you do have a blender, place all other ingredients into the blender. Select low speed. Turn machine on and quickly increase speed to medium. Run for 15–20 seconds or until the ingredients are well mixed. Stop machine and use a spatula to remove the mixture. **Enjoy!**

Natural Hair Conditioner

Makes 14 ounces
Total time: 25 minutes
Ingredients:

1 Mashed Ripe Avocado *(medium sized)*
1 cup Parsley
1 cup Banana
1 tablespoon Coconut or Olive Oil
1 teaspoon Jojoba, Grape Seed, or Almond Oil
½ teaspoon Molasses
1 tablespoon Dairy-Free Yogurt or Soy-Free Veganaise
1 teaspoon Lemon Juice
½ teaspoon Cayenne
4 – 6 Drops Essential Oils. Select three (3) from the four (4) listed below:
Lavender, Rosemary, Tea Tree or Peppermint Oil.
2 tablespoons Bulk Herbal Teas: Select 1 teaspoon each from four (4) out of seven (7) herbal teas listed below:
Chamomile, Calendula, Nettle, Marshmallow, Rosemary, Burdock Root or Dandelion

Directions:

Put tea in two cups of water. Bring to boil. Let tea steep for 20 minutes. While tea is steeping, place all other ingredients into blender. Strain tea. Add 1 cup of strained herbal tea to the other ingredients in the blender. Blend all ingredients until smooth.

Pour conditioner in a jar with a lid or top or in a clear condiment squeeze bottle. Squeeze and massage it throughout your hair and scalp. After you are done, cover your hair with a plastic cap. Leave conditioner on hair for 30–60 minutes or overnight. It works well on gray hair too.

Hemp/Basil Dressing

Prep time: 20 minutes
Makes 3½ Cups
Ingredients:
½ cup soaked Sunflower Seeds (presoaked for at least 2 hours)
1 cup Coconut or Olive oil
1 cup Water
½ cup Lemon Juice
½ cup chopped Parsley
½ cup chopped Basil
½ cup Cilantro
1 teaspoon chopped Shallots
1 tablespoon chopped Jalpeno Pepper
1 tablespoon Bragg Liquid Aminos or Shoyu

1 cup Hemp Seeds
¾ teaspoon salt
1 teaspoon Dill Weed
1 teaspoon Oregano
½ teaspoon Chipotle
½ teaspoon Cayenne

Directions:
Place all ingredients into blender. Start at low speed and gradually increase until smooth. If there is no blender, mix well. Serve immediately or refrigerate.

Enjoy!

Hemp Milk

Prep Time: 10 minutes
Makes 2 Cups
Ingredients:

½ cup Hemp Seeds
2 cups Water
2 Medjool Dates
½ teaspoon Vanilla
½ teaspoon Cardamom
½ teaspoon Cinnamon

Optional:
1 tablespoon Raw Cacao
½ teaspoon Allspice
½ teaspoon Nutmeg
½ teaspoon Iris Moss

Directions:

Place all ingredients in blender on high speed for 20 seconds. Optionally, you can strain the mixture through messbag or cheesecloth to remove the seed particles. The seed particles can be refrigerated for use in other recipes or put in cereal, pancakes, waffles, smoothies, soup or stew. Serve immediately or refrigerate in an airtight glass container for up to 3–5 days.

Kale Chips

Prep 10 minutes
Cook 7–8 minutes
Ingredients:

2 tablespoons Olive Oil
Liquid Braggs Amino

Chipotle	Paprika
Cumin	Shallots
Turmeric	1 bunch Curly Kale (Dinosaur optional)
Italian Seasoning	2 large cookie sheets or pans
Cayenne Pepper	Mineral or Sea Salt

Directions: Preheat an oven to 450 degrees F (232 degrees C). Thoroughly soak Kale in a large bowl with cold water with a dash of Sea Salt to remove grit and discourage little critters. Rinse off Kale in cold water.

Carefully remove the leaves from the stems of the Kale. Thoroughly dry kale with a paper towel or a salad spinner and cut into bite size pieces.

Massage and rub each kale piece with the Olive Oil on the cookie sheets or pans.

Sprinkle with seasoning to taste. Rub and massage spices on the Kale.

Place Kale in the oven. If more than one oven rack is used for the two pans or cookie sheets (one above the other), after 3 minutes, switch the Kale on the top with the Kale on the bottom. Keep in oven for the remaining time. Check it after 5 minutes.

Bake until the edges are brown, but not burnt, 5 to 7 minutes.

Simple Kale Stir-Fry

Total Time: 18 min
Prep: 10 min
Cook: 8 min
Ingredients:

3 tablespoons Coconut or Olive Oil
¼ cup chopped Shallots
¾ cup chopped Scallions
1 bunch Kale with leaves torn, stalks discarded, coarsely chopped.
1 tablespoon Turmeric
¼ teaspoon Mineral or Sea Salt
1 teaspoon Cumin
¼ teaspoon Cayenne

Instructions: Thoroughly soak kale in a large bowl with cold water with a dash of Sea Salt to remove grit and discourage little critters. Rinse off kale in cold water. Tear the leaves from the stalks, coarsely chop kale leaves.

Heat oil in a large skillet or wok over medium heat with Scallions, Shallots, Salt, Turmeric, Cayenne and Cumin. Stir it around 2–3 minutes so it won't burn. Add Kale and stir around 3–5 minutes. Remove cooked dish to a plate and serve!

Optional: Serve with Quinoa, Pasta, Black, Red, or Brown rice.

Lasagna with Basil Cashew Cheese

Prep Time 1 Hour
6–8 Servings
Cooking Time 35–45
Makes 1 9x13 Pan
Basil Cashew Cheese Topping:

¼ cup Raw Cashews (soak in 1 cup of water for 30 minutes)

Pour the 1 cup of Water containing the Soaked Cashews into the blender or food processor.

2 ½ tablespoons Tapioca Starch

1 cup – fresh Basil

¼ teaspoon Mineral or Sea Salt

1 tablespoon Oil (Olive or Coconut)

½ cup Nutritional Yeast

1 teaspoon fresh Lemon Juice

¼ cup chopped Scallions

Add all ingredients into a high-powered blender or food processor and blend until smooth. Pour topping into a small saucepan and cook. Continue to stir over medium high heat. After a few minutes the mixture will start to look like its curdling or separating. Reduce heat to medium and continue stirring so you don't burn the bottom of the saucepan.

Keep cooking and stirring until the mixture gets real thick and becomes like melted dairy cheese. In about 2–3 more minutes, remove from heat and let it cool. As soon as it has cooled enough pour the topping into a container. Cover the container and place it in the refrigerator for later use.

The Sauce or African Stew (page 341)

Lasagna with Basil Cashew Cheese | 81

Lasagna Sauce Ingredients:

1 tablespoon Coconut or Olive Oil
¼ teaspoon Mineral or Sea Salt
¼ cup chopped Scallions   1 teaspoon Turmeric
¼ chopped Shallots   ½ teaspoons dried Basil
½ teaspoon Oregano   2 cups Salsa (medium or mild)
½ teaspoon Thyme   1 teaspoon Maple Syrup
1 Vegetable Bouillon cube

Sauté the scallions and shallots in oil for 1–2 minutes in a saucepan on medium heat. Add the other ingredients. Reduce the heat to low and let it simmer, stirring occasionally for 5 –10 minutes. Remove from heat.

Plant Protein Filling:

2 cups Raw Sunflower Seeds   **Optional:**
5 oz Kalamata or Black Olives   ½ cup Carrots
½ cup chopped Shallots   1 teaspoon Italian Seasoning
½ cup Lemon or Lime Juice   ¼ teaspoon Ginger Root
½ teaspoon Mineral or Sea Salt   ¼ cup chopped Celery
1 teaspoon Turmeric   ¼ teaspoon Chipotle
½ teaspoon Basil   2 tablespoons Cilantro
1 tablespoon Sesame Seeds
1 cup chopped Scallions
1 tablespoon Cumin
2 tablespoons Parsley
½ cup Beets
¼ teaspoon Cayenne Pepper
½ cup Bell Pepper
2 tablespoons Tomato
2 tablespoons Oil (Coconut or Olive)

Put Sunflower seeds into food processor. Pulse seeds until semi-smooth and set them aside in a bowl. Put salt, shallots and olives in processor using the S-blade until smooth. Combine Sunflower seeds and add all other ingredients with the oil and blend until semi-smooth.

Lasagna

Vegetable Stir-fry

Ingredients:

2 tablespoon Oil (coconut or Olive)
1 chopped Scallions
2 tablespoons chopped Shallots
1 cup Zucchini (chopped)
½ cup sliced Mushrooms
1 cup Spinach
1 cup Kale
1 box of Brown Rice Pasta or Lasagna Noodles

Optional:

¼ teaspoon Cayenne
½ cup Red Pepper
¼ cup chopped Ginger
¼ cup chopped Shallots
1 teaspoon Soy Free Chick-pea Miso
½ teaspoon Mineral or Sea Salt

STEP 1– Preheat oven to 375°Fahreheit (190 Celsius).

Optional to Sauté seeds: Caraway, Fennel, Cumin and Coriander in large skillet, wok or pan before sautéing shallots, bouillon cubes and shallots in oil over low-medium heat for 3-5 minutes.

Otherwise, sauté scallions, bouillon cubes and shallots in oil over low-medium heat for 2-3 minutes. Add Zucchini and Mushrooms, sauté for 2-3 more minutes. Add Kale and Spinach and sauté for additional 2-3 more minutes.

Optional to add: Cabbage, Asparagus, Carrots, Parsley, Cilantro, Basil or Tomato

Optional to Sprinkle: Ground Turmeric, Cumin, Tarragon, Thyme, Oregano, Rosemary, Fenugreek, Sage, Marjoram

STEP 2 – Cook 1 box of brown rice pasta or lasagna noodles. Check the box directions for boiling pasta or noodles. Generally, add 3–4 quarts water. Bring water to rapid boil. Add ½ teaspoon mineral or sea salt to reduce sticking. Lower heat to low and add noodles 2–3 pieces at a time and stir. Return to rapid boil. Cook uncovered while stirring for 3–4 minutes with brown rice pasta or 8–10 minutes with lasagna noodles, stirring occasionally. Watch lasagna or pasta to prevent over cooking. Drain pasta or noodles well in strainer or colander. Pour cold water over noodles or pasta to cool and prevent sticking. Separate cooked lasagna or pasta and lay on wax paper.

STEP 3 – Layer the Lasagna: Pour about a cup of sauce or African stew into a 9×13 inch pan and spread it evenly. Add a layer of sautéed vegetables. Then add another layer of pasta or noodles. Then, spread sauce on top of noodles or pasta along with the plant protein filling. Add another layer of pasta or noodles.

STEP 4 – Repeat layers of sauce and plant protein filling. Then, add a layer of sautéed vegetables. Add basil cashew cheese topping. Optional to sprinkle herbs and spices: ground turmeric, cumin, tarragon, thyme, oregano, rosemary, fenugreek, sage, marjoram or cayenne

STEP 5 – Bake for 35–45 minutes, watching closely so as not to burn the edges.

Tasty Millet

Makes 6–8
Cooking Time:
25–30 minutes

Millet is gluten free and a good source of fiber. The main grain in China before rice, it has a sweet nutty flavor. Considered to be one of the most digestible and non-allergenic grains available, it is high in protein and antioxidant activity. Importantly, millet hydrates the colon to keep you from being constipated. It is one of the few grains that are alkalizing to the body. It contains magnesium that can help reduce the effects of migraines and heart attacks. The serotonin in millet is calming to moods.

Ingredients:

1 cup Millet

2 cups Water

¼ teaspoon Mineral or Sea Salt

¼ teaspoon ground Cinnamon

1 teaspoon Turmeric

Optional:

¼ teaspoon Allspice

¼ teaspoon ground Ginger

Directions:

Boil 2 cups of water adding salt, cinnamon and turmeric for 3–5 minutes. Pour in millet and stir. Turn heat to low, cover and let millets simmer 25–30 minutes, stirring occasionally to avoid burning the bottom of the pot or pan. Remove from heat, Stir, uncovered 15–20 minutes to let the grains separate. Eat, enjoy!

NaaCereal

Makes 6–8 Servings
Cooking Time: 30–35 Minutes
For Infants or Adults
Ingredients:

2 cups water

1 cup grains: Select four of the five grains below.

Add ¼ cup of each:

Steel Cut Oats, Millets, Quinoa (Black, Red, Beige or Tri–color),

Black Forbidden Rice or Red Rice

1 teaspoon Olive or Coconut oil

1/8 teaspoon Mineral or Sea Salt

Select four (4) out of the seven (7) spices:

1/8 teaspoon ground Cinnamon

1/8 teaspoon Mace

1/8 teaspoon Turmeric

1/8 teaspoon Nutmeg

1/8 teaspoon Cardamom

1/8 teaspoon Sage

1/8 teaspoon Cloves

Fruits: Select desired fruit from those listed below equaling one cup. Seasonal fruit is best.

Oranges	Strawberries	Pears
Pineapple	Blueberries	Persimmons
Bananas	Apples	Kiwi

Super–foods

¼ teaspoon Chia seeds	¼ teaspoon Nutritional Yeast
¼ teaspoon Ground flax seeds	1 large Date

¼ teaspoon Pea Protein   1 tablespoon Raisins

Wet Ingredients:

½ cup to taste: Water, Almond or Hemp milk

Cooking Directions:

Boil 2 cups of water adding oil, salt and spices for 3–5 minutes.

Pour in grains and stir. Turn heat to low, cover and let grains simmer 25–30 minutes, stirring occasionally to avoid burning the bottom of the pot or pan. Remove from heat. Stir the grains and leave uncovered 10–15 minutes to let the grains separate.

Place in blender, Vita–mix, Nutra bullet or Baby Ninja

1 cup grains

1 cup Fruit

½ cup or to taste: Water, Almond or Hemp Milk

Super–foods

Blend course or puree, depending on the ability of child or adult to chew.

• See Almond and Hemp milk recipes

NaaCereal Non–Infant Formula

Optional: Non Infant Formula:

After cooking grains and allowing them to separate, place grains in bowl with fruit, water, almond or hemp milk and super–foods. Stir and eat.

Quinoa, Black and Red Rice Mix

Serves 6–8
Cooking Time: 45 minutes

Quinoa is gluten free. It has been called "The Mother" of all the grains. One of the most protein–rich foods we can eat, it is a complete protein containing all nine essential amino acids. It contains almost twice as much fiber as most other grains. Fiber helps to relieve constipation and prevent heart disease by reducing high blood pressure and diabetes. Fiber lowers blood sugar levels and cholesterol and may help you to lose weight.

It has a good amount of iron, which helps keep our red blood cells healthy and increases brain function. It contains lysine, which is essential for tissue repair and growth. It is rich in magnesium, which helps to relax blood vessels and thereby alleviate migraines. It also contains Manganese, which is an antioxidant, which helps to protect red blood cells and other cells from injury by free radicals.

Ingredients:

- 2 cups Water
- ¼ teaspoon Mineral or Sea Salt
- ¼ teaspoon ground Cinnamon
- ¼ teaspoon Cumin
- ¼ teaspoon Thyme
- ¼ teaspoon Cayenne powder
- ½ cup Quinoa
- 1 teaspoon Turmeric
- ¼ cup Red Rice
- ¼ cup Black Rice
- 1 vegetable bouillon cube

Optional:

- ¼ teaspoon ground Shallots
- ¼ teaspoon ground Parsley
- 3 Cardamom Seeds
- ¼ teaspoon Saffron

Directions:

Boil 2 cups of water adding salt, cinnamon, turmeric, cumin, thyme and cayenne for 3–5 minutes. Pour in quinoa, black and red rice, stir. Turn heat to low, cover and let grains simmer 25–30 minutes, stirring occasionally to avoid burning the bottom of the pot or pan. Remove from heat. Stir, leave uncovered 15–25 minutes to let the grains separate. Eat, enjoy!

Real Banana Pancakes

8–10 Pancakes
Prep time 15 minutes
Cook time 40 minutes
Ingredients:
¾ cups Buckwheat Flour
¾ cups Quinoa Flour
(optional) Spelt, Amaranth, Rye, Coconut
1 teaspoon Nutritional Yeast
½ teaspoon Baking soda
1 tablespoon Flax Seeds (ground)
1½ teaspoons Baking Powder (aluminum free)
½ teaspoon Cinnamon
½ teaspoon Mineral or Sea Salt
1 tablespoon Maple Syrup or Coconut Nectar
1 cup Almond or Hemp milk
1½ Bananas (medium sized)—mash into mix
¼ cup Coconut (Olive) Oil
(optional) Top with strawberries, mango, blueberries or other fruit

Directions:
Mix flour, baking powder, baking soda, cinnamon, salt and flax seed, into a medium–large bowl.

Whisk the bananas, milk and oil together in a medium–large bowl.

Make a well in the center of the dry ingredients, and pour in the wet. Stir or use blender until mixture is smooth

Wipe the surface of the griddle, skillet, or pan with the oiled napkin or paper towel.

Heat the lightly oiled griddle, large non-stick skillet, or frying pan over low medium heat.

Drop 1/4 cup of batter onto a hot oiled griddle, or well-greased frying pan or skillet over medium high heat.

When bubbles appear on the surface of the pancake, approximately 3 minutes, flip, and cook until browned on the other side for another 2 minutes.

Drop another 1/4 cup of batter onto the hot oiled griddle, well greased frying pan, or skillet

Repeat with remaining mixture until the batter is gone. Enjoy!

Pineapple Rind Drink

Prep Time: 10 minutes
Serves 4–6
Cook Time: 35–40 minutes
Ingredients:
1 Medium Pineapple
4 cups Water
Directions:
Rinse pineapple and remove rind and core
Cut rind and core into strips or pieces
Place water and pineapple rinds into pot

Bring water to medium high and boil covered for 35–40 minutes
Remove pot from heat
Keep lid on pot
Let pineapple drink steep for 30–60 minutes
Remove pineapple rind and strain
Serve immediately or refrigerate.
Can store refrigerated for 2 weeks. Enjoy!

Pizza

Prep Time: 1 hour
Cook Time: 10–15 minutes
Makes 12 –16 Slices
The pizza is made in 5 parts:
The basil cheese topping, crust, African Stew or sauce, plant protein filling and raw salad.
First, you'll need to make the

Basil Cashew Cheese Topping:

¼ cup Raw Cashews (soak in 1 cup of water for 30 minutes)
Pour the 1 cup of Water containing the Soaked Cashews into the blender, or food processor.

2 ½ tablespoons Tapioca starch	1 cup fresh Basil
¼ teaspoon Mineral or Sea Salt	1 tablespoon Oil (Olive or Coconut)
½ cup Nutritional Yeast	
¼ chopped Shallots	1 teaspoon fresh Lemon Juice

Add all ingredients into a high-powered blender or food processor and blend until smooth. Pour topping into a small saucepan and cook. Continue to stir over medium high heat. After a few minutes the mixture will start to look like its curdling or separating. Reduce heat to medium and continue stirring so you don't burn the bottom of the saucepan.

Keep cooking and stirring until the mixture gets real thick and becomes like melted dairy cheese in about 2–3 more minutes. Remove from heat and let it cool. As soon as it has cooled enough pour the topping into a container. Cover the container and place it in the refrigerator for later use.

The Crust:
2 cups Quinoa or Barley Flour
1 teaspoon Mineral or Sea Salt
Buckwheat or Spelt Flour
1 teaspoon Maple Syrup
2 tablespoons Dry Yeast (1 packet)
1 tablespoon Coconut or Olive Oil
½ cup Flax Seed
1 cup warm Water

Combine all ingredients in a large bowl and stir to create dough. Add additional flour to dough as needed to keep dough from sticking to bowl or to hands. Place dough on slightly floured flat surface and knead for 10 minutes. This means, to press, massage or squeeze the dough with your hands blending the mixture together. If the underside or bottom of dough is sticking to the surface, pull up dough and add additional flour and re-knead. Repeat process until the underside or bottom of dough no longer sticks. Knead dough into a half rounded ball or dome shape. Place dough in a large bowl and cover to let it rise in a warm place for 60 minutes while you complete the other parts of the pizza.

The Sauce: Use 2–3 Cups of African Stew or Pizza Sauce:
1 tablespoon Coconut or Olive Oil
¼ teaspoon Mineral or Sea salt
¼ cup chopped Scallions
1– teaspoon – Turmeric
¼ cup chopped Shallots
½ teaspoons dried Basil
½ teaspoon – Oregano
2 cups Salsa (medium or mild)
½ teaspoon Thyme
1 teaspoon Maple Syrup
1 Vegetable Bouillon Bube

Sauté the shallots and scallions in oil for 1–2 minutes in a saucepan on medium heat. Add the other ingredients. Reduce the heat to low and let it simmer, stirring occasionally for 5 –10 minutes. Remove from heat.

Plant Protein Filling

Makes about 2 Cups

2 cups – Raw Sunflower Seeds

5 oz Kalamata or Black Olives

½ cup chopped Scallions

¼ cup Lemon or Lime Juice

½ teaspoon Mineral or Sea Salt

1 teaspoon Turmeric

½ teaspoon Basil

1 tablespoon Sesame Seeds

1 cup chopped Scallions

1 tablespoon Cumin

2 tablespoons Cilantro

2 tablespoons Parsley

Put Sunflower seeds into food processor. Pulse seeds until semi-smooth and set them aside in a bowl. Put salt, shallots and olives in processor using the S-blade until smooth. Combine Sunflower seeds and all other ingredients with the oil and blend until semi-smooth.

Raw Vegetables: Sprinkle vegetables on top of Pizza.

¼ cup Cilantro

¼ cup Tomatoes

¼ cup thinly sliced Cauliflower

¼ cup fresh Basil

¼ cup thinly sliced Broccoli

Optional:

¼ cup chopped Celery

¼ cup chopped or thinly sliced Scallions

2 tablespoons thinly sliced Daikon

¼ cup shredded Cabbage

¼ cup Bell Pepper	2 tablespoons Olives
¼ cup Parsley	¼ cup Kale
¼ cup chopped Pineapple	2 tablespoons Carrot (grated)

Putting The Parts Together: Preheat the oven to 500 Fahrenheit (260 Celsius).

When dough is ready after 60 minutes, roll out dough on a floured surface as thick or thin as you desire. Spread pizza with the Pizza Sauce or African Stew. Then spread the Plant Protein Filling on top of the Sauce or African Stew. Sprinkle the Raw Vegetables on top of the Filling. Add drops of the Basil Cashew Cheese Topping on top of the pizza.

Bake pizza on a slightly oiled baking sheet for 10–15 minutes or until the crust is nicely browned. If desired, sprinkle pizza with additional fresh chopped Basil, ground Oregano, Cayenne or Paprika after is comes out of the oven. Eat! Enjoy!

Spicy Vegan Plantain

Prep Time: 10 minutes
Serves 4–6
Cook Time: 20–25 minutes
Ingredients:
4–6 very ripe Plantains
½ cup Raisins
1 teaspoons Cinnamon
½ teaspoon Cloves
1 teaspoon Nutmeg
¼ cup chopped Pineapple
4 tablespoons Oil (Coconut or Olive)
1 teaspoon Allspice
½ teaspoon Mace
½ tablespoon chopped Ginger
Optional:
½ cup dried unsweetened Cranberries
½ cup Blueberries

Directions:

Peel plantain and cut into thin slices. Heat oil in large skillet or wok. Place over medium low heat and sauté the plantain in a single layer. When golden on the bottom, turn plantain over with spatula. Add nutmeg, cloves, cinnamon, allspice, mace, pineapple and ginger. Stir continuously until plantain begins to caramelize.

Serve immediately and enjoy!

Tasty Polenta

Serves 6–8
Cooking Time: 15 minutes

Polenta is made from corn, grains and legumes. It is gluten-free. A good source of fiber, it originated as a peasant food in Northern Italy. Freshly made polenta from whole-grain corn can supply long-lasting energy and has the consistency of grits. It is considered easy to digest. It contains good amounts of magnesium, iron, thiamine, phosphorus and zinc. The zinc contributes to a healthy immune system.

The complex carbohydrates in corn help slow the rate of glucose absorption, thereby controlling blood sugar levels. It is a good source of Vitamins A and C, which benefit cancer and heart disease prevention. It can also be made into cakes for frying or grilling. Since, today's corn is almost entirely genetically modified, use only organic polenta.

Ingredients:

2 cups Water
¼ teaspoon Mineral or Sea Salt
¼ teaspoon ground Paprika
1 teaspoon Turmeric
1 teaspoon ground Cardamom
1 teaspoon Thyme
½ teaspoon Basil

Optional:
¼ teaspoon Saffron
½ Vegetable Bouillon cube
¼ teaspoon Parsley

Directions: Boil 2 cups of water adding salt, paprika, cardamom, basil, thyme and turmeric for 3–5 minutes. Pour in polenta and stir. Turn heat to low, cover and let polenta simmer 15–20 minutes, stirring occasionally to avoid burning the bottom of the pot or pan. Remove from heat. Stir, leave uncovered 15–20 minutes to let the grains separate. Eat, enjoy!

Portobello Mushrooms

Prep Time: 10 minutes
Cook Time: 20 minutes
Serves 4
Ingredients:
4 Portobello mushroom caps
¼ cup Bell Pepper
2 tablespoons freshly chopped Mint
¼ cup Coconut or Olive Oil
1 cup chopped Tomatoes
3 tablespoons chopped Scallions
3 tablespoons chopped Shallots
1 teaspoon finely chopped Rosemary
2 teaspoons Bragg Liquid Aminos
½ teaspoon Mineral or Sea Salt
½ teaspoon Cayenne
2 tablespoons fresh Lemon or Lime Juice

Optional:
1 tablespoon Balsamic

Directions:
Preheat oven to 400 Fahrenheit (204 Celsius)

Clean mushrooms and remove stems, reserve stems for other recipes. Place the mushroom caps on a plate with the gills up. Use a spoon to remove gills. In a small bowl, combine the rosemary, cayenne, scallions, tomatoes and shallots. In another bowl combine oil, juice, salt and Bragg.

Bush over both sides of mushroom caps with the oil, juice, salt and Bragg mixture. Spoon the mixture of rosemary, cayenne, scallions, shallots and tomatoes evenly into each mushroom cap. Place mushrooms on baking sheet or dish. Place the baking dish on middle rack in the oven. Bake for 20 minutes. Serve immediately.

Tasty Potato Salad

Serves 6–8
Cooking Time: 25 minutes
Ingredients:
3 lbs Potatoes
(Yukon, Red or Purple)
(About 8 medium sized)
Finely chopped:
3 tablespoons Parsley
¼ cup fresh Dill Weed
¼ cup Dinosaur Kale
¼ cup Bell Peppers
¼ cup Beets
½ cup Broccoli
¼ cup Cilantro
¾ cup chopped Scallions
¼ cup Cucumber
1 teaspoon Chipotle
1 tablespoon Oregano
1 tablespoon Water
1 tablespoon Pea Protein
2 tablespoons Olive Oil
2 tablespoons Maple Syrup or Coconut Nectar
2 tablespoon Mustard
2 teaspoons Lemon or Lime Juice
1 teaspoon ground or fresh Basil
1 tablespoon Mineral or Sea Salt
1 tablespoon Turmeric
¼ cup Olive oil
2 tablespoons Bragg Liquid Aminos
Optional:
¼ cup Red Cabbage

¼ cup Cauliflower
¼ cup Celery
1 Tomato sliced on top
¼ cup fresh Fennel
½ teaspoon Paprika
1 teaspoon Marjoram
½ teaspoon Cayenne
½ cup Olives

Directions:

Wash potatoes with skin on. Cut potatoes into quarter or eights. Place in large pot. Fill pot with water over the level of the potatoes. Boil potatoes with skin on medium heat for 20 minutes or until tender. Squeeze juice from lemon or lime in a small bowl.

After boiling, place potatoes in a large bowl. Add: All vegetables, herbs, seasoning, mustard, lemon or lime juice, Bragg, maple syrup and olives into large bowl with the potatoes. Stir well. Sprinkle ½ teaspoon lemon juice on top. Eat. Enjoy!

Pulp Burger/Juice

Makes 10–12 Open faced Sandwiches & about 2 quarts Juice
Juice Ingredients:

4 Apples	½ bunch Kale
3 Oranges	4 Celery Stalks
1 Pear	1 cup Pineapple
½ cup Dandelion	2 Beets (medium sized)
1 Daikon	3 Cucumbers (medium sized)
½ cup Parsley	
¼ cup chopped Ginger	
2 Carrots	
½ cup Cabbage	

Burger Ingredients:
Catsup, mustard, sliced cucumber (pickles), shallot, grain bread, 4–6 beds of lettuce, 1 sliced tomato, 1 avocado

Directions:
1. Rinse all items.
2. Remove stems and cut seeds out of apples, oranges and pears.
3. Juice all items.
4. Collect pulp from juiced items.
5. Toast bread.
6. Spread catsup, shallot, avocado and mustard on toasted bread.
7. Spread pulp evenly on top of catsup, mustard and avocado.
8. Place thinly sliced cucumber (pickles), shallot and sliced tomato on top of pulp.

Raw Ice Cream

Prep Time: 5 min.
Serves 4–5
Ingredients:
1 cup frozen Blueberries
1 cup frozen Strawberries
3 frozen ripe Bananas
2 cups Almond or Hemp Milk
¼ cup Maple Syrup or Coconut Nectar or to taste

Optional:
1 teaspoon Vanilla Powder

Directions:
1. Blend the frozen strawberries with milk until semi-smooth.
2. Add the frozen bananas, blueberries and blend until creamy.
3. Serve immediately or store in the freezer.

Raw Salad

Prep Time: 40 minutes
Serves 8–12
Ingredients:

1 cup Carrots
¼ cup Cilantro
½ cup chopped Cauliflower
1 cup sliced Collar Greens
¼ cup Parsley
½ cup Celery
¼ cup chopped Zucchini
1 cup Swiss Chard
1 cup Spinach
1 cup chopped Beets
¼ cup Basil
1 cup Napa Cabbage
¼ cup Mint
1 cup chopped Broccoli
¼ cup Fennel
¼ cup Dill Weed
1 cup Dinosaur Kale
1 cup Purple Kale
1 cup Beet Greens

Optional:
¼ cup chopped Asparagus
¼ cup Green Beans (seasonal)
¼ cup dried Seaweed
1 cup chopped Cucumber
½ cup Boc Choy
½ cup Leeks
¼ cup Brussels Sprouts
¼ cup Daikon

Directions: Pour the following vegetables into a large bowl and toss.

Vegan Real Waffles

12 –14 Waffles
Prep time 15 minutes Cook time 30 minutes
Ingredients:
¾ cups Buckwheat Flour
¾ cups Quinoa flour (optional) Spelt, Amaranth, Rye, Coconut
1 teaspoon Nutritional Yeast
½ teaspoon Baking soda
1 tablespoon Flax Seeds (ground)
1½ teaspoons Baking powder (aluminum free)
½ teaspoon Cinnamon
½ teaspoon Mineral or Sea Salt
1 tablespoon Maple Syrup
1 cup Almond or Hemp milk
1½ Bananas (medium sized)—mash into mix
¼ cup Coconut or Olive oil

Optional:
Top with strawberry, mango, blueberries or other fruit.
Mix flour, Nutritional Yeast, baking powder, baking soda, cinnamon, salt and flax seed, into a large bowl.
Whisk or mix the bananas, milk and oil together in a medium-large bowl.
Make a well in the center of the dry ingredients, and pour in the wet. Stir or use blender until mixture is smooth
Preheat the waffle iron per the machine's instructions.
Brush the waffle iron with oil (Coconut or Olive). Use a paper towel or pastry brush to oil both the bottom and top plates of the waffle iron. Repeat this process of oiling the plates before you make each waffle, or it is most likely that the waffles will stick to the plates.

Spoon in, depending on the waffle iron, about ¼ – ½ cup of batter evenly into the bottom plate of the waffle iron and close to cook.

The first waffle will be the tester. So, if you have poured in too much batter, not enough or more oil is needed to avoid sticking, you can make the adjustments for the next waffle.

Close the lid and wait until the waffle iron's indicator light shows that cooking is complete, or until no more steam comes out. This may be 3–5 minutes, depending on the waffle iron. The cooked waffle should be crispy and golden brown.

Remove the waffle with a spatula or butter knife to help you lift it without burning your fingers or breaking the waffle. Place the cooked waffle on a plate or place the cooked waffle in a 200 degree Fahrenheit (93 Celsius) oven until serving. Oil the plates and pour more batter into the waffle iron to make another waffle. Repeat until all the batter is gone.

Roasted Eggplant Vegetable Casserole

Cooking time: 50 Minutes
Serves 2–4 For 3–4 Days
Ingredients:

2 (medium sized) Eggplants
2 tablespoons Sesame Seeds
¼ cup finely chopped Shallots
¼ cup chopped Ginger Root
1 teaspoon Parsley
1 teaspoon Chipotle
2 large Tomatoes
1 cup Bell Peppers
¼ cup Broccoli
½ teaspoon Mineral or Sea Salt
1½ cup Kale
½ cup fresh Mint
¾ cup Coconut or Olive oil
2 tablespoons Bragg Liquid Aminos
1 cup chopped Scallions
2 tablespoons Lemon or Lime Juice
½ teaspoon Cayenne
1 Glass Jar Salsa (12 oz) or 1½ cup African stew

2 teaspoons Oregano
1 teaspoon Thyme
1 teaspoon Rosemary
1 teaspoon Cumin
1 cup fresh Basil
1 teaspoon Turmeric
¼ cup chopped Beets

Directions:

Preheat oven 450 Fahrenheit (232 Celsius). Grease bottom of large Pyrex or Baking pan (13x9 pan) with oil. Cut 2 Eggplants (medium) in half the long way. Slice each half into ½ inch cuts. Place Eggplant in bottom of pan.

Pour ½ cup Oil on Eggplant. Massage Oil on both sides of Eggplant. Sprinkle Bell Peppers and Shallots on top of Eggplant. Slice 2 large Tomatoes and one cup chopped Scallions on top of Eggplant.

Sprinkle Turmeric, Cumin, Mineral or Sea Salt, Chipotle, Rosemary, Cayenne, Thyme, Parsley, Oregano, Mint, Ginger, Basil, Sesame Seeds, Broccoli, Kale, Lemon or Lime Juice and Beets on top of Eggplant. Pour ¼ cup of Oil and Bragg on Casserole. Add either African Stew or Salsa on top.

Place in oven for 25 minutes at 450 Fahrenheit (232 Celsius). Remove from oven. Turn Eggplant over in Pyrex or pan. Place Eggplant back into oven for another 25 minutes. Check to see if skin of eggplant is soft. If eggplant skin is not soft, bake up to an additional 20 minutes in the oven. Take Eggplant out of oven. Eat, enjoy!

Salad Dressing

Ingredients:
3 tablespoons Water
1 teaspoon Turmeric
1 tablespoon Pea Protein
1 tablespoon Hemp Seeds
1 tablespoon Organic Shoyu
¼ cup Bragg Liquid Aminos
1 tablespoon finely chopped Shallots
½ teaspoon Mineral or
Sea Salt or to taste
1 teaspoon Organic Braggberry
¼ teaspoon Cayenne
2 tablespoons Olive Oil
¼ cup Lemon or Lime Juice
1 teaspoon Sesame Seeds

Optional:
1 teaspoon Fig Balsamic Vinegar
¼ teaspoon Thyme
¼ teaspoon Paprika
¼ teaspoon Chipotle

Directions: In medium bowl

Add: All ingredients. Mix ingredients and pour in jar or bottle. Use immediately on salad or refrigerate.

Steel Cut Oats

Serves 6–8

Cooking Time: 45 minutes

Steel-cut oats are gluten free. They are the inner portion of the oat kernel which has been cut into two or three pieces. They differ from rolled oats, which have been flattened, steamed, rolled, re-steamed and toasted. Due to this additional processing, rolled oats lose some of their natural taste, nutritional value, texture and fiber.

Steel-cut oats are an excellent source of protein, fiber, rich in B-vitamins and calcium, while low in unsaturated fat and sodium. Steel-cut oats help eliminate fat and cholesterol from the body. This translates to lower cholesterol and a decrease in the risk of developing diabetes, cancer and heart disease.

Ingredients

1 cup Oats
2 cups Water
¼ teaspoon Mineral or Sea Salt
¼ teaspoon ground Cardamom
1 teaspoon Turmeric
¼ teaspoon ground Cinnamon
¼ teaspoon ground Cloves
½ teaspoon Allspice
1 teaspoon Coconut Oil

Optional:

¼ teaspoon ground Ginger
¼ teaspoon ground Nutmeg
¼ teaspoon ground Mace

Directions:

Boil 2 cups of water adding coconut oil, salt, cinnamon, cloves, allspice and turmeric for 3–5 minutes. Pour in oats and stir. Turn heat to low, cover and let oats simmer 25–30 minutes, stirring occasionally to avoid burning the bottom of the pot or pan. Remove from heat. Stir, leave uncovered 15–20 minutes to let the grains separate. Eat, enjoy!

Baked Sweet Potatoes/Yams

Prep Time:
10 minutes
Cook Time: 1 hour
Serves 4–6
Ingredients:
9x13 dish
4 large sweet potatoes or yams
Coconut or Olive oil

Directions:
1. Preheat oven to 400 Fahrenheit (204 Celsius).
2. Wash the sweet potatoes/yams and pat dry with a paper towel.
3. Lightly grease pan.
4. Lightly massage oil on the skins of the sweet potatoes/yams.
5. Use fork to pierce skin of potato in three (3) places.
6. Bake at 400 degrees for approximately an hour, or until tender.
7. Check potatoes/yams and rotate periodically to evenly cook.

Quinoa Tabouli

Serves 6–8
Cooking Time: 45 minutes
Ingredients:
1 cup Quinoa
2 cups Water
1 Vegetable Bouillon Cube
½ cup Shallots
1 teaspoon Turmeric
1 teaspoon Bragg Liquid Aminos
1 teaspoon Mineral or Sea Salt
½ teaspoon Cayenne Pepper
1 teaspoon Cumin
3 tablespoons Olive Oil
3 tablespoons Lemon Juice
1 cup chopped fresh Mint leaves
2 cups diced Tomatoes or Cherry Tomatoes halved
1 cup chopped Parsley Leaves
1 cup chopped Cilantro
½ cup chopped Green Onions
2 cups diced Cucumbers
Optional:
¼ cup Dandelion
¼ cup chopped Jicama
¼ cup chopped Cauliflower

Directions:

Boil 2 cups of water adding dash of salt, ground cumin, turmeric, cayenne pepper and 1 bouillon cube for 3–5 minutes. Pour in Quinoa and stir. Turn heat to low, cover and let quinoa simmer 25–30 minutes, stirring occasionally to avoid burning the bottom of the pot or pan. Remove from heat. Stir, leave uncovered 15–20 minutes to let the grains separate. Refrigerate 30–60 minutes.

In a large bowl, pour Quinoa, chopped herbs and vegetables, oil, Bragg, lemon juice and salt. Mix well. Chill, serve and enjoy.

Feel free to add additional spices...Mix well.

Mixed Spiced Tossed Salad

Prep Time: 15 minutes
Serves 8–10
Ingredients:
1 Head Romaine Lettuce (cut up or torn)
3 cups Spring Mix Salad

Dressing:
¾ cup Olive oil
¼ cup chopped Parsley
½ cup Water
½ cup Lemon Juice
1 cup chopped Shallots
1 teaspoon Cumin
1 teaspoon Bragg Liquid Aminos or Shoyu
¼ teaspoon Turmeric
2–4 un-pitted Medjool Dates
1 tablespoon Chick Pea Miso
1 teaspoon Oregano

Directions:
Blend dressing mixture in blender until creamy and smooth.

Make Topping:
1 teaspoon Chia Seeds
1½ cup Pine Nuts
2 tablespoon Flax seed or Omega Twin oil
1 teaspoon Mineral or Sea Salt

Pulse topping mixture in blender or food processor until coarsely chopped.

Toss spring mix and lettuce with dressing. Sprinkle topping mixture on top and serve.

Enjoy!

Variety Fruit Salad

Prep Time: 25 minutes
Serves 10–12
Choose 10 out of the 14 fruits below:
1 cup Apple
1 cup Blueberries
1 cup Banana
1 cup Oranges
1 cup Pineapple
1 cup Cherries
1 cup Strawberries
1 cup Mango
1 cup Raspberry
1 cup Grapes
1 cup Guava
1 cup Blackberries
1 cup Kiwi
1 cup Pear

Optional:
Persimmon, Peach, Apricot, Fig, Nectarine, Plum and Papaya. Add Almond, Hemp Milk to taste.

Directions:
Fruit is seasonal. If certain fruits are not available simply substitute other fruits. Mix fruit.

Sprinkle the below Power Boosters to taste:

Flax seed, Cacao, Raisins, Dates, Almonds, Mulberries, Goji Berries, Prunes, Hunza Berries, Hemp Seeds, Chia Seeds, Maca, Spirulina, Psyllium Husk, Moringa Powder or Iris Moss Powder.

Refrigerate all fruit salad that is not used for another day or other recipes.

Made in the USA
Las Vegas, NV
07 August 2024